SECTORAL ANALYSIS OF TRADE, INVESTMENT AND BUSINESS IN VIETNAM

Sectoral Analysis of Trade, Investment and Business in Vietnam

Edited by

Tran Van Hoa
Associate Professor of Economics
University of Wollongong
Australia

380.109597
S446

 First published in Great Britain 1999 by
MACMILLAN PRESS LTD
Houndmills, Basingstoke, Hampshire RG21 6XS and London
Companies and representatives throughout the world

A catalogue record for this book is available from the British Library.

ISBN 0–333–71683–3

 First published in the United States of America 1999 by
ST. MARTIN'S PRESS, INC.,
Scholarly and Reference Division,
175 Fifth Avenue, New York, N.Y. 10010

ISBN 0–312–21762–5

Library of Congress Cataloging-in-Publication Data
Sectoral analysis of trade, investment and business in Vietnam /
edited by Tran Van Hoa.
p.   cm.
Includes bibliographical references and index.
ISBN 0–312–21762–5 (cloth)
1. Vietnam—Commerce.   2. Vietnam—Economic conditions.
3. Industries—Vietnam.   4. Investments—Vietnam.   5. Vietnam–
–Foreign economic relations.   I. Tran, Van Hoa.
HF3800.5.Z5S43   1998
380.1'09597—dc21   98–23860
                                                                CIP

This book is printed on paper suitable for recycling and made from fully managed and
sustained forest sources.

10   9   8   7   6   5   4   3   2   1
08   07   06   05   04   03   02   01   00   99

Printed and bound in Great Britain by
Antony Rowe Ltd, Chippenham, Wiltshire

To my loving wife
Souraya
and my loving daughters
Danielle and **Cybele**

Contents

Acknowledgements

This book is the third in a series of books on the spectacular achievements in economic development attained in recent years by the countries in South East Asia in particular and in the Asia Pacific Economic Co-operation (APEC) region in general. We are committed to prepare and publish in our triennial (1995–7) university–industry research project to satisfy the demand from a wider readership interested in these achievements and the prospects arising from them for use in studies in trade, investment, business and other commerce. The readership we are aiming at includes the business community (corporations and individual investors), government trade agencies, chambers of commerce and industry, and other institutions, academics, economic advisers, business economists, management and strategic consultants. It is also intended for students of international trade, business and economic development who, during the course of their investigation and planning, require a well researched, soundly analytical and quantitative assessment of the available emerging market, market size, structure and pattern of consumption, production and finance, significant trends, competitiveness and business opportunities.

The research for the book was carried out during 1996 as part of our work for the project *Foreign Investment in Vietnam*, which has been funded partly by the Australian Research Council of the Department of Employment, Education and Training and partly by the Vietnam Institute for Trade (formerly the Research Institute for Foreign Economic Relations, the Ministry of Trade) for the triennium 1995–7. The researchers and contributors to the book are experts in their own right in their own country who, fortunately for us, have agreed to collaborate to provide us with an authorirative survey and reliable forecasts of the issues, problems, solutions, and opportunitites for trade, investment, and business in Vietnam for use or reference by all interested persons, be they local or ·foreign. For its main objective, the book is focused specifically on sectoral or industry-by-industry analysis, and to meet this targeted scope, it covers in detail the conditions (as well as possible obstacles) of supply, demand, finance, law and trade for all twenty sectors of the economy of Vietnam, from agriculture and rural development to private, foreign direct investment and official (governmental) development assistance.

During the preparation of the book, I have benefited from the help and assistance of colleagues in the Department of Economics and the Research Institute for International Business at the University of Wollongong, and from discussions with senior members of the NSW Vietnam Chambers of Commerce. I have had great help, understanding and encouragement in many forms from my wife Souraya and daughters Danielle and Cybele during the writing and editing of this book.

TRAN VAN HOA

Notes on the Contributors

Kim Van Chinh is an expert in the Ministry of Science-Technology and Environment, Vietnam.

Dang Ba Lam is Director at the National Institute for Education Development in Hanoi.

Nguyen Anh Dung is a consultant to the ICTC, Vietnam Institute for Trade, Ministry of Trade.

Nguyen Anh Tuan is a Doctoral Candidate at the National Administration Institute in Hanoi.

Nguyen Cong Hoa is an expert at the Institute of Information Technology, Hanoi.

Nguyen Dung is an expert in Vietnam's General Department of Post and Telecommunications in Hanoi.

Nguyen Gia Kim is a senior expert in the Ministry of Trade, Vietnam.

Nguyen Khac Than is Director of the World Economics Institute, Hanoi, Vietnam.

Nguyen Khac Thanh is a consultant to the ICTC, Vietnam Institute for Trade, Ministry of Trade.

Nguyen Tien Nhuan is Director of the Institute for Land Management, Hanoi.

Nguyen Trung Que is Professor at the Institute of Agriculture, Ministry of Agriculture and Rural Development in Hanoi.

Nguyen Van Thach is an expert in the Ministry of Industry, Vietnam.

Pham The Tho is Chief of the Trade Information Department, Vietnam Institute for Trade, Ministry of Trade.

Pham Van Khoi is an Associate Doctor at the National Economics University, Hanoi.

To Ngoc Thanh is an engineer at the Ministry of Construction in Hanoi.

Vu Tuan Canh is Director of the General Department of Tourism, Hanoi.

1 Sectoral Analysis of Trade, Investment and Business in Vietnam

Tran Van Hoa

INTRODUCTION

With the emergence of Vietnam as a major (even though, currently, a developing and transitional) economy in the Association of the South East Asian Nations (ASEAN) in particular and in the Asia Pacific Economic Co-operation (APEC) region in general, the trading countries of the world have taken a keen interest in this new and important change. This interest arises from the fact that Vietnam is a country in an early stage of economic development, a huge market of 76 million people (as at 1996), with vast untapped physical, natural and human resources, the achievement of spectacular output growth rates since the introduction of Doi Moi (renovation) in the mid-1980s, a fast-rising income per head, and a conspicuous consumption tendency. In addition, Vietnam is geographically situated at the hub of important sea and land routes in South East Asia, linking the subcontinent in the west, Oceania in the south, and the largest and some of the richest and most advanced countries in the world in the north and the north-east. Strategically and politically, Vietnam is, within a 2000 km radius, at the centre of activities in the neighbouring regions, and a buffer zone for any potential disputes, large or small, between the continental mass of Central Asia and Eastern Europe and the Indian and Pacific oceans.

These characteristics of Vietnam make it economically, politically and strategically one of the most favoured

1

countries in Asia for the development of trade, investment and business, as well as for co-operation and alliance.

In the area of trade, investment and business (TIB for short), a number of books have been published dealing with its macroeconomic and international or global aspects. These books are concerned mainly with the big picture, which is relevant to economic issues of globalization and internationalization. But, in practical investigations of TIB to formulate policy or to develop commerce and trade for small and medium-sized enterprises, or even for giant corporate conglomerates, a detailed study, sector-by-sector, is necessarily appropriate and therefore desirable. This book meets this criterion, and the sectors (from agriculture and rural development to banking and finance, public administration and even official development assistance by international organizations and countries) covered by it is sufficient for a competent study of each of the important sectors making up the complete economy of Vietnam.

The sectors dealt with in the book comprise, more specifically:

Chapter 2   Agriculture and rural development, including the main exports of paddy rice and other primary produce and products.

Chapter 3   The construction industry and its crucial role in the development of the country via construction, investment, commerce, labour supply and the use of new technology.

Chapter 4   Education and training, youth affairs, the problems of educational reforms and the policy of reskilling of the workforce, and of fostering talents during the transition period of the country's development.

Chapter 5   Energy (coal, electricity, oil and gas) as a driving force of economic development and a main export income (helping the country's trade balance and hard currency problems). Major programmes on energy and their implications for the economy and foreign investment are also discussed.

Chapter 6   Banking as well as other financial operations and relevant legal documents supporting these operations are discussed and their implications and strategies given.

Chapter 7   Current problems with forest logging and potential from forestry for the economy in Vietnam and international trade are discussed. Wood reserves and prospects for reforestation and regreening of the land are also surveyed and analyzed.

Chapter 8   Information technology (IT) as a priority development programme of the government of Vietnam with an emphasis on machinery and equipment, the labour force and training is analyzed. Applications of IT to public administration and finance are also discussed.

Chapter 9   Land management (forest land use, special purpose land use and residential land) together with its impact on food production, ecological and environmental preservation aspects, and the ensuing difficulties encountered are studied.

Chapter 10   Vietnam's mineral, oil and gas reserves and their supply (exploitation, beneficiation and contracts) and demand conditions are reported, and prospects for investment assessed.

Chapter 11   Post and telecommunications and their operation and future demand and supply are evaluated and suggestions made for development and investment.

Chapter 12   Privatization as one important instrument of economic reforms in Vietnam with structural, legal and training implications for small and medium-sized enterprises is discussed.

Chapter 13   Conditions for and targets (law, machinery, cadres contingent or public servants) of reforms in public administration with an objective of having a workforce capable of the proper management of modernization and industrialization are analyzed.

Chapter 14   Science and technology development since 1945 and its current status in fundamental and social sciences as well as its training target and possible personnel and legal problems are dealt with.

Chapter 15   Tourism for both local and international visitors as an important sector of Vietnam's economy (revenue, employment) together with planned future development and related environmenal issues is discussed.

Chapter 16   Transport and communication (land, water, sea, river, aviation and railways) throughout the country and development strategies are surveyed.

Chapter 17   Vietnam's radio and television industry including its present situation in terms of needs and supply (transmission and state budget) and future plans is investigated and evaluated for development and investment.

Chapter 18   Vietnam as an ASEAN member implies a certain relationship and suggests several implications for international trade, investment, business and other regional co-operation. Present and future directions from this dynamic change are analyzed.

Chapter 19   Vietnam's labour force and its allocation to industries from its 76 million people in 1996 and a projected approximately 85 million people in 2000 are discussed with a view towards improving human resource development for industrialization and modernization of the country and to provide acceptable social security systems in the long term.

Chapter 20   This chapter details the scope of study, issues and problems in official development assistance to Vietnam since the days of the former USSR to the Western and newly-industrialized countries at the present time. Suggestions for a more effective use of ODA in future donations, and their management and allocation, are also given.

Chapter 21 Sums up the whole book.

In all the chapters, the main structure for analysis follows a theme, examining the situation of supply and demand in the various sectors of Vietnam's economy in the past, at the present time, and likely trends and issues to the year 2000, or even to 2020. Based on these trends, what will be the required investment (both private and public), co-operation and ensuing opportunities for international corporations, overseas individual investors and business people? This kind of analysis provides information necessary to proper TIB planning and development for these interested groups. In the case of overseas governmental financial assistance and official legal documents that are necessary for development, promotion, operation and protection of international TIB activities, the theme is: what is the required assistance and action by international organizations and the foreign government sector to assist in Vietnam's economic development and in promoting local and international TIB activities in Vietnam for the benefit of both the local and international business communities.

The wealth of information and its authoritative and sound analysis given in the following chapters will, we hope, provide the fundamentals for TIB development, promotion, operation and management in Vietnam for the business community worldwide, for mutual economic and social benefits in the medium term and in the long run. For readership outside the business community, the chapters will, we hope, provide necessary information for academic studies or for issues and problems that are inherently fundamental and crucially related to international business and trade as well as to important aspects of economic development and transition.

2 Vietnam's Agriculture and Its Prospects to 2000

Nguyen Trung Que

GENERAL BACKGROUND

Vietnam has the specific characteristics of an agricultural country, with 80 per cent of the population living in the countryside and 72 per cent of the total workforce participating in agricultural production activities. As a result, Vietnam has, in the past, always put an emphasis on agriculture, considering it to be the most important area of production. Thanks to the renovation policy, Vietnam has, from the status of a rice importer, now not only satisfied the domestic consumption demand but also exports a volume of between 1.5 and 2 million tonnes of rice annually. Some other exported products include coffee, rubber, fruits and vegetables. Vietnam's agriculture is now being developed intensively under the orientation of diversifying products, fully exploiting the potential and strengths of a tropical monsoon agricultural country.

The 1988–90 period was an important milestone, marking a strong growth rate for agriculture, with a cultivation output reaching 19.5 million tonnes in 1988 and climbing to 20.5 million tonnes in 1989. Vietnam's agriculture, has been shifted gradually from a self-sufficient situation to commodity production, with the proportion of food in circulation reaching over 40 per cent of the total output. The value of exported agricultural–forestry–aquatic products was US$800 million in 1990, nearly 60 per cent of the total export turnover, and this figure increased to US$1.276 billion in 1992.

7

An increase in the volume and value of exported agricultural products has made an important contribution to the stabilization of the economy, politics and society, thereby considerably improving the lives of Vietnamese farmers.

The 1990–2 period was a time when the structure of the rural economy moved under the orientation of developing industry, handicrafts and services, transferring redundant labour from agriculture into the industrial and handicraft fields and thoroughly exploiting the potential of forestry and aquatics. As compared with the 1990–2 period, the 1993–5 period saw an increase of 9 per cent of per capita food output (324 kg per capita) and a 31 per cent increase in exported rice. Vietnamese rice has now been on sale in France, the USA, Japan, Singapore, Hong Kong, Indonesia, the Philippines, Malaysia, Iraq and South Korea. Vietnam exported 1.73 million tonnes of rice in 1993 and 2.15 million tonnes in 1995. Thus the security of the food industry is firmly assured. However, there is still a problem; that is, the big difference in prices between agricultural and industrial goods which has not encouraged agricultural producers. The share of agriculture in GDP will be reduced in the future. Attention has been paid to investment in agricultural product processing, especially processing frozen meat and fresh fruits and vegetables for export. The volume of processed meat exports was 12.2 million tonnes in 1993 and reached approximately 20 million tonnes in 1994. Frozen meat was mainly exported to ASEAN countries.

EXPORTING OF AGRICULTURAL PRODUCE

Vietnam's agricultural produce export market has expanded continuously, one of the country's main exports being rice. Between 1991 and 1995, Vietnam became the third largest rice exporter in the world. Vietnamese rice was sold at a relatively low price in foreign markets: US$191–228 per tonne in 1994 and up to US$240–250 per tonne in 1995. This resulted from the fact that the world rice market is very ebullient and the quality of Vietnamese rice has increasingly been improved. It has been forecast that rice demand in China will increase that and Vietnam will pay special attention to the export of its rice to this market.

Coffee is Vietnam's second most important agricultural export. In the 1991–5 period, Vietnam exported nearly 700 000 tonnes of coffee. Vietnamese coffee is exported to twenty countries, of which Singapore accounts for 50 per cent, the Federal Republic of Germany for 10 per cent, and Hongkong for 8 per cent of Vietnam's total quantity of exported coffee. Vietnam has now turned to the European Union and North American countries for its foreign coffee market. Because of the increase in the production of coffee and its export to many countries, the price of Vietnamese exported coffee has been affected strongly and has had a tendency to fall. The price of exported coffee was US$2500 per tonne in 1992–3 and at times to as low as US$680–800 per tonne. The price of one tonne of Vietnamese coffee sold in foreign markets is often US$50–200 lower than the international price. The prospect for Vietnam's coffee prices for 1998 seems good, however, as Brazil experienced bad weather conditions in the first half of 1997.

Rubber is also a very important export item (mainly sold in the form of dry latex). In 1995, Vietnam exported 110 000 tonnes of latex.

Included in the list of items with the largest export turnover in Vietnam are aquatic products, which will become a key export item in the future. In the 1991–5 period, the average export turnover growth rate of this group was more than 35 per cent annually. Vietnam's aquatic exports rank 19th and 30th in terms of quantity and turnover respectively in the world, and have been sent to a total of 25 countries, mainly Japan (with a 60 per cent share of the total), regional reprocessing markets (20 per cent), and Western European, North American and Australian markets (15 per cent). However, these products have not yet established a firm ground in the world market at large.

Vietnam has now attached great importance to investing in, expanding and developing some other agricultural exports such as tea, pepper, cashew nuts, peanuts, vegetables and so on, which have enjoyed the confidence of the global market and will increase both in terms of quantity and the proportion of the total export turnover.

AGRICULTURAL FIELDS IN NEED OF FOREIGN INVESTMENT IN VIETNAM

For the present, foreign investment plays an important role in the economic development in Vietnam, especially in the transformation of agricultural production into finished product or commodity production. So far, there have been 137 foreign projects in this industry with the total capital of US$541 million (accounting for 4.5 per cent of the total investment capital in Vietnam), of which there are eighty-five projects in the agricultural–forestry field worth US$396 million, and fifty-two projects in the aquatic products field, worth US$145 million.

One noticeable thing is that these projects often require a relatively large amount of capital (because of poor infrastructure, outdated equipment and low-quality production materials used in agriculture in Vietnam) but the profit ratio is low and the pace of capital recovery is also slow. Unlike industrial production, agricultural production in Vietnam depends a lot on natural conditions and, as a consequence, investments in this field often suffer from risks caused by natural changes. In addition, the investment environment in Vietnam is still in the process of being established, therefore it cannot help but cause difficulties for investors. For example, the legal system is inconsistent, and administrative procedures are cumbersome. These have the effect of influencing adversely the attraction of investment capital to the field of agriculture.

Currently, the government of Vietnam is giving top priority to projects in agriculture, especially those concerning agricultural product processing and food technology, among others.

FORECAST FOR VIETNAM'S AGRICULTURE AND PROSPECTS

There is a common recognition among agricultural policymakers in Vietnam that Vietnam's agricultural exports have achieved an important increase in terms of quantity in recent years, but their prices in the world market are low because most of these products only go though primary processing, and do not have a reputation for high quality. Some examples are seed coffee and latex. Twenty-five per cent of the total aquatic product output is exported to regional reprocessing markets.

It has been conceded that the situation has resulted from a poor rural infrastructure, and a shortage of agricultural– forestry–aquatic products processing facilities, leading to a post-harvest loss that is estimated at about 15 per cent of the total output. Vietnam's processing establishments own outdated equipment and technologies, thus the quality of processed agricultural products is low and cannot yet satisfy the demands of the world market. Facilities serving production have degraded and have not received much investment. As a consequence, they cannot meet the requirements of production development, and limit the possibility of specialization and product saleability.

Some projected targets for Vietnam's agriculture up to the year 2000 are as follows:

1. Food and foodstuffs output will reach between 30 and 32 million tonnes (2 to 2.5 million tonnes of rice will be for export).
2. Output of processed meat of all kinds will increase from 1.8 to 2 million tonnes.

3. Sugar output; 1 million tonnes; kernel coffee: from
    220 000 to 240 000 tonnes; rubber: from 180 000 to
    200 000 tonnes; and dry tea: 70 thousand tonnes, with
    a total export turnover of US$3.5 billion.

To this end, Vietnam will have to work out solution to
expand the agricultural product consumption market, and
establish specialized agricultural areas in fields such as
aquatic cultivation and breeding, and the planting of fruit
and vegetables for export.

Currently, Vietnam has attached great importance to
investing in processing technologies and is calling for
foreign capital investment in this field in order to turn out
competitive products in an open economy. At a time when
Vietnam has joined ASEAN and extended its relationship
with the APEC and the WTO, domestic agricultural producers and processing enterprises have focused on the
expansion of Vietnam's agricultural product market to
these countries.

The present situation and the future development of
Vietnam's agriculture will provide a lot of prospects for
Australian and other investors, especially those investing
in agricultural and aquatic-product processing technologies. At present, some Vietnamese goods such as crude oil,
textiles and aquatic products have been sold to Australia,
but in a very small amounts.

In order to accelerate bilateral economic co-operation,
Australia needs to pay prime attention to Vietnam's agriculture and give first priority to investment in food technologies. Vietnam is still facing a big problem concerning
the processing and preservation of rice goods in the largest
rice-growing area of the Mekong (Cuu Long) river delta.
In this region, there is an annual production surplus of
2 million tonnes of rice which suffer losses or devaluation
because of the absence of drying technologies and changes
in the weather. There have been some instances when the
rice of the previous harvest has not all been sold or appro-
priately preserved before the crop from the next harvest-
ing season arrives. This continuing cycle has forced

farmers to sell off the old stock, and this is one of the reasons that has brought Australian investors to Vietnam, wishing to invest in Vietnam's agricultural sector.

In the later 1990s, co-operation between Vietnam and Australia in agriculture has not been extensive but has helped to boost Vietnam's agriculture to some extent. The Australian Council for International Agricultural Research (ACIAR) and the government of Vietnam have signed collaboration and assistance agreements on nine research projects in the fields of husbandry, veterinary medicine, botanical preservation, and plant strains. Many Vietnamese scientific researchers have attended various training courses in Australia. Australia has also invested in the milk-cow husbandry and milk processing areas in the northern part of Vietnam. Negotiations to establish similar projects in the southern part of Vietnam are being completed. A joint venture producing interior woods was established in 1990 and is now operating well, with an annual turnover of US$1 million.

In addition to the import of Australian technologies and equipment, Vietnam also buys some agricultural products, such as canned food, vegetables and so on from Australia. In future, if Australian investors invest in processing aquatic products, meat, fruits, vegetables and in clean-vegetable growing areas, they can gain a high economic efficiency and returns as the raw materials for processing are readily available in Vietnam.

CONCLUSION

Vietnam enjoys a great many comparative advantages in agricultural production. Exports of agricultural produce account for 50 per cent of the country's total export turnover. Vietnam can supply Australia with many products such as rice, tea, coffee, rubber and aquatic products, to name just a few. Vietnam's agriculture is now badly in need of capital for modernization, and Australia can co-operate in terms of supplying technologies, equipment and help with exports from the sector. What need to be done now is for the two sides to make contact and work out long-term and overall strategies to stimulate bilateral co-operation and increase mutual social and economic benefits in the two countries.

3 Vietnam's Construction Industry: Prospects for Foreign Investors

To Ngoc Thanh

GENERAL BACKGROUND

In parallel with the fast economic growth rate in the economy, in the 1986–95 period, Vietnam's construction industry notched up considerable growth, averaging between 21 per cent and 30 per cent annually. The construction output value in the five years 1986–90 was VN$3356 billion (equal to US$333 million), and soared to VN$36 150 billion (equal to US$3.6 billion), showing an increase of 10.8 times in the 1991–5 period.

In the five years between 1991 and 1995, Vietnam mobilized approximately VN$206 550 billion (equal to US$18.65 billion) from all capital sources in the whole of society for development investment, of which the contribution from the state budget, state credit funds and state enterprises was VN$95 740 billion, accounting for 46.35 per cent; that from the public was VN$64 500 billion, accounting for 31.23 per cent; and that from foreign direct investment VN$46 340 billion, accounting for 22.4 per cent. The investment capital scale was enlarged and increased through the years, with increases of 11.9 per cent, 27.2 per cent, 43 per cent and 30 per cent in the years 1991, 1992, 1993, 1994 and 1995, respectively, when compared with the preceding year.

Thanks to fast growth of investment capital, especially foreign direct investment capital, in the ten years 1986 to 1995, many construction works have been put in place, such as Hoa Binh hydroelectric power station with a capacity of 1920 MW; Thac Mo hydroelectric power station with a capacity of 150 MW; Vinh Son hydroelectric power station with a capacity of 66 MW; Northern Thang Long-Noi Bai highway; Tan Son Nhat runway; and some export processing zones and focal industrial zones such as those of Trung Linh (Ho Chi Minh City), Sai Dong (Hanoi), Ninh Thuan (Song Be province) and so on.

The construction material industry has developed equally quickly. The 1976–85 period saw an average annual growth rate of 10 per cent, holding a share of 13 per cent of the investment capital for industries and 6 per cent of the total investment for the whole national economy. The average annual growth rate of the industry was 15 per cent in the 1986–94 period, and climbed to 20 per cent in 1995. To date, there have been twenty-eight foreign projects in the exploitation, production and business of cement, construction steel, ceramic tiles, porcelain sanitary wares, glass and so on. with a total investment capital of US$1.5 billion. Cement production in the 1986–90 period reached 23.497 million tonnes, annually supplying the construction market with between 5 and 6 million tonnes. Also in that period, production of porcelain sanitary ware, enamelled or glazed tiles, construction glass, bricks and construction stone increased by 15.1 times, 8.6 times, 11.6 times, 1.35 times and 1.1 times, respectively, over the previous period.

As for construction steel, Vietnam has been able to satisfy two-thirds of total domestic demand. The renovation has brought about a great many changes in the housing field in Vietnam. The average annual growth rate of house-building is 35 per cent. At the time of writing, the average area per person in urban areas has increased to 5.8 sq.m. (compared with 4.35 sq.m. per person in 1990).

VIETNAM CONSTRUCTION DEMAND TO 2000

In order to reach the target of industrializing and modernizing the country and doubling gross domestic product

(GDP) per capita by the year 2000, Vietnam will need to mobilize an investment capital amount of about VN$450 000 billion (equal to US$41.3 billion), of which 51 per cent (that is, US$21.3 billion) will be mobilized from the domestic economic sectors and the rest from foreign direct investment (FDI).

The FDI sources will be allocated for the following fields:

- Developing the oil and gas industry under the target to exploit about 20 million tonnes of crude oil by the year 2000, completing the construction of an oil refining factory before the year 2000, and another one after the year 2000. The total investment capital will be about US$7.5 billion.
- Building two high-tech industrial zones in Hanoi and Ho Chi Minh City, with a capital amount of about US$600 million.
- Establishing twelve focal industrial zones in Ho Chi Minh City, Hanoi, Haiphong, Dong Nai, Song Be, Can Tho, Quang Nam–Da Nang and Hai Hung with an estimated capital amount of approximately US$5 billion.
- Investing around US$2 billion in light industry.
- Setting up heavy industrial enterprises in the fields of metallurgy, mechanics, electronics and chemicals, with a capital of about US$1.5 billion.
- Building 5–6 cement factories with a total output of 9–10 million tonnes per year in Ha Tien, Hai Phong, Hai Hung, Quang Ninh, Quang Nam–Da Nang and the Northern Nghe An, with a capital of US$1.5 billion.
- Developing the agricultural, forestry, fishery and processing industries, with a capital of about US$800 million.
- Investing US$1 billion in transport, communications, telecommunications and infrastructure.
- Building hotels, offices for rent and tourism resorts with a capital of about US$1 billion.
- Investing US$300 million in services.

Construction Materials Industry

The cement output is targeted to reach 20 million tonnes per year by the year 2000. To that end, in addition to the construction of some more new factories, there is a need to invest in increasing the production capacity of existing factories.

Great importance has been attached to the development of porcelain sanitary ware and tile production. By the year 2000, the annual production capacity of enamelled or glazed tiles should reach 15–18 million sq.m.; porcelain sanitary ware, 2.5 million units; construction glass, 60 million sq.m.; standard bricks, 12 billion pieces; and construction steel, 1 million tonnes.

House Construction Industry

By the end of 1995, the total housing area in use in Vietnam was about 500 million sq.m., of which the area in urban centres was about 81 million sq.m., accounting for 16 per cent. The average housing area per capita was 7 sq.m. in the whole country, 7.5 sq.m. in the rural areas and 5.8 sq.m. in urban centres, which are concentrated in two large cities, Hanoi and Ho Chi Minh City (the former accounting for 8 per cent and the latter 44 per cent).

It is forecast that by the year 2000, because of the natural growth rate of the population, there will be about 20.5 million people living in urban centres. In order to satisfy the minimum housing demand of 8 sq.m. per capita, the total housing area in urban centres should reach 164 million sq.m., up 83 million sq.m. over the present requirement with an annual increase of 16.6 million sq.m., that is 20 per cent of the total existing area. This is an ambitious target which will require a high level of capital investment.

Industrial Construction

The purpose of Vietnam's construction development strategy is to turn the country into an industrialized nation, which necessitates a great demand for investment in industrial construction. Up to the year 2000, priority will be given to the development of oil and gas exploitation and processing; petrochemicals; energy projects such as Yaly and Song Hinh (Hinh River) hydroelectric power stations; Phu My and Hiep Phuoc thermal power stations; twelve export processing and high-tech industrial zones, and so on. It is estimated that by the year 2000, there will be 30–40 focal industrial zones in Vietnam.

Other Construction Works

Vietnam is now implementing an outward-orientated development strategy. The increasing number of foreigners coming to Vietnam for business and tourism purposes has generated a high demand for offices, houses and hotel rooms. At the time of writing, Vietnam has about 2335 hotels, with a total number of 50 000 rooms, that are up to international standards. It is forecast that by the year 2000, there will be 3.5–4 million foreign tourists coming to Vietnam, and about 11 million local tourists. These figures are predicted to be 8–9 million and 25 million by the year 2010. Therefore, up to the year 2000, 25 000 more rooms should be built and 5100 more rooms built each year subsequently. At the present cost of US$4000–6000 per room, Vietnam will need US$60–90 million per year for investment.

Vietnam is one of the countries with the poorest infrastructure in the world. Therefore, the government has attached great importance to upgrading and building new transport and communication works, seaports and airports. The projects of upgrading the national highway 1A and the Hanoi–Haiphong Highway No. 5 are being carried out. Projects to improve the North–South railway, and to build a new railway from Ho Chi Minh City to Phnom Penh are also planned. As for seaports, the target is to increase the handling capacity from 20 million tonnes to 55–60 million tonnes by the year 2000, and 130–150 million tonnes by the year 2010. At present, sea transportation can only satisfy 45 per cent of the export–import carrying demand.

In the coming years, investment will be focused on the construction of such ports as Haiphong, Saigon, Danang, Cailan, Dungquat and Chivai-Vungtau. Regarding airports, the government has approved a project to upgrade the Noibai airport, with a total investment of US$150 million. Other airports, such as Tan Son Nhat and regional airports, are also badly in need of improvement and enlargement.

The construction demand up to the year 2000 in Vietnam will be very high. According to estimates by the Ministry of Construction, the total construction output value would be VN$30 000–35 000 billion each year. In order to meet the construction demand, besides the attraction of foreign and local investment capital, there need to be an rearrangement of the organizational structure, courses for training construction engineers, renovation of management, and modernization of equipment and machinery in the construction industry.

PROSPECTS FOR FOREIGN INVESTMENT IN CONSTRUCTION

Investments

According to statistics from the Ministry of Planning and Investment, total operational foreign investment capital during 1988–95 was about US$7735 million, of which investment capital in 1994 was US$1700 million and in 1995 US$4500 million. As for the construction industry, in the 1991–5 period, there were thirty-two projects concerning water supply and drainage financed by grants or loans from foreign countries and international organizations; nine research projects in the fields of management, science, technology and training; and thirty joint-venture projects, of which there were six projects on cement production, ten on construction and assembly; and six on consulting or manufacturing. Of total investment capital in Vietnam, the construction industry accounted for 8 per cent in the 1988–94 period, with 11 per cent in 1994 alone.

Commerce

In recent years, Vietnam's construction material industry has developed rapidly and, step by step, has satisfied the great demand for construction. However, Vietnam still has to import annually a great quantity of high-quality building materials from abroad. Main imports are cement (1 million tonnes per year); flooring tiles (1–1.4 million sq.m. per year); porcelain sanitary ware (380 000–400 000 units); construction glass (11–12 million sq.m. per year); and construction steel (500 000 tonnes per year). In addition, Vietnam also has to import electric and water equipment, aluminum frames, and construction equipment such as drilling machines, bulldozers and so on.

Highly competitive foreign building companies in Vietnam's construction material market come from China, Taiwan, Thailand, Malaysia, Italy, Spain, and other countries.

Number of Employees

At the time of writing, there are 700 000 employees working in the construction field, of which 300 000 work in 750 state-owned large and small enterprises. Most domestic construction works are undertaken by the local workforce, with technical assistance from foreign partners in some essential phases.

However, the local workforce has not been well trained, and working tools are very poor and of only basic design and standards. There is, therefore, a need to organize training courses to improve the professional skills of the workforce. Vietnam is also badly in need of excellent construction designers and planners.

Technology

In the 1996–2000 period, Vietnam will need US$500–1000 million to renovate construction equipment such as foundation-laying equipment, digging machines (rolling and lifting), cranes, and to supply pumping machines and means of transport to industrial factories specializing in manufacturing steel structures for concrete mixing. This amount of capital will be mobilized from foreign direct investment.

In Vietnam, priority is given to foreign investment projects in the fields of infrastructure construction, heavy industrial development, export processing zones, high-tech industrial zone construction, hotel and office-for-rent construction, and tourism. Therefore, the construction demand in coming years will be very high. At the time of writing, many foreign companies have invested in the production of construction materials, especially cement, tiles, construction glass, aluminum, steel, stone exploitation and so on.

Some Australian investors have also been present in Vietnam in the construction field. Up to now there have been four Vietnam–Australia joint ventures. They are: the Mekong raw concrete manufacturing factory; a venture specializing in the design, building and development in Ho Chi Minh City; the Hai Van-Thiess construction venture, also producing concrete for the Southern area; and housing construction in Hanoi.

Vietnam has imported construction materials from Australia, such as porcelain sanitary ware, water pipes, construction equipment such as concrete pumping machines, concrete mixing trucks and some accessories for the HaTien cement production line. Regarding co-operation in the construction field between Vietnam and Australia, there have been bilateral ministerial-level visits, and dialogues between investors, consultants, attorneys and contractors of the two countries.

Vietnam is now a huge construction site and the demand for construction up to the year 2000 will be very high.

Australia is able to co-operate with Vietnam in a great number of construction fields, the most important ones including construction material production, design and planning, building technologies, and consulting in terms of construction bidding and tendering.

4 Education and Training in Vietnam: Development Orientations to 2020

Dang Ba Lam

EDUCATION AND TRAINING IN VIETNAM : BRIEF HISTORY AND CURRENT STATUS

Vietnam is located in South East Asia, covering a land area of 331 700 square kilometres; in 1996, its population was 76 million.

In spite of a low per capita income of US$270 in 1995, the literacy rate was high – 89 per cent. This is a great achievement, taking into account the fact that in 1945 – at the end of French colonization – 95 per cent of the population was illiterate. The achievement is even more remarkable given the enormous difficulties facing education and training (ET) under the dramatically changing context of Vietnamese society over the last fifty years.

In the period 1987–96, the renovation of ET as an important part of socioeconomic and political changes has continued to take place in Vietnam. In fact, this process started in 1979 – several years after the reunification of the country, when Vietnam entered a new stage of reconstruction after forty years of war. Obviously, there were great challenges and expectations placed upon ET. However, these challenges were in conflict with the real situation of ET. They were: the increasing rate of drop-out among schoolchildren; the decreasing scope of vocational, secondary, professional and higher education; the serious reduction of resources; and the decline in motivation and qualifications among teachers. As a result, the quality of ET went down and could not meet the demands of society.

Besides these disadvantages caused by war, the situation can also be explained by the bureaucratic, centrally-planned mechanism adopted prior to 1987. As ET activities were determined, implemented and funded by the state plans only, creativity and flexibility of the educational institutions were limited, and available resources of the whole society were not fully mobilized for ET development.

The turning point for society in general, and ET in particular, occurred in 1986, when the decision to become market economy was taken at the 6th Congress of the Vietnam Communist Party. This political change may have some implications for the development strategy of ET: ET should meet diversified demands of all economic sectors, but not just of the state; ET is funded not by the state alone; and ET should incorporate the principles of a market mechanism. The place of ET was redefined as 'a driving force of social development'.

The priority to be given to ET was reaffirmed by the 7th Congress of the Vietnam Communist Party held in 1991, when it was stated that:

> Education is considered as the first national priority policy, as the driving force and the basic condition in ensuring the realization of the socio-econonic objectives, and of building and defending the Fatherland.

In the light of this new approach, the objectives of ET have been redetermined as:

- Increasing the educational level of the whole population;
- Training the manpower necessary for development; and
- The nurturing of talents.

Following these guidelines, some important measures have been implemented to improve ET, namely:

- The system of ET has been restructured to be more comprehensive and flexible, to meet diversified demands of different client groups and communities, as well as to be compatible with educational systems in the world.
- The network of ET institutions has been reorganized in order to make the best use of the available intellectual and material potential. In parallel with the state sector, non-state institutions are being established to meet social demand. The process of amalgamation of higher education institutions is going on. Because of diversifying forms of training, the scale of ET has been expanded. The number of students at all educational levels has increased: to compare with 1990–91, in the 1995–6 school year, the number of preschool, general, vocational and higher education students grew by 1.3, 1.28, 1.22 and 2.87, respectively. Considerable progress has been made towards eradicating illiteracy and universalizing primary education through the implementation of the Law on Universalizing Primary Education. The universalizing of lower-secondary education has been implemented in the more developed areas of twenty provinces and cities.
- Quality of ET has been enhanced by such measures as improving content and methods of teaching and learning; diversifying upper-secondary education into three streams on an experimental basis; renovating the process of university training into two phases; and updating or introducing new subjects.
- Some improvement in teaching staff's morale has been achieved by introducing such incentives as awarding honour titles, classifying teachers by different levels, and encouraging their professional development.
- The budget for ET has been increased by such measures as introducing systems of tuition fees, encouraging entrepreneurial activities of ET institutions, and mobilizing funding from other sources.

In short, over the period 1987–95, under conditions of limited resources, some initial progress of ET has been made. However, there are still some limitations: objectives, content and methods of ET have not fully satisfied the demands of socioeconomic renovation; its quality and effectiveness are still low; the scale of education in less developed areas is small; the qualifications of teaching staff are poor; and educational management is irrelevant. There are several critical issues facing ET that require urgent solutions.

First, there is still a considerable gap between the capability of the ET system and the requirement to improve its quality. This may be explained not only by the lack of funding given to update infrastructure as well as teaching and learning facilities, but also by inefficient utilization and management of available existing resources.

Second, teaching staff are irrelevant to the requirements of renovating teaching programmes and methods; motivation and commitment to their jobs are low. The lack of an appropriate incentive and rewarding mechanism may be one of the reasons leading to such a situation.

Third, ET is not really congruent with practice. So far, the mechanism of making an educational plan on the basis of clients' needs has not been established. Thus, ET cannot meet the real needs of the practice effectively, and social contributions to ET cannot be mobilized as fully as they should be. This is because the renewal of ET management is slow, and hence cannot follow the changes of a market mechanism. There is a lack of legislation defining responsibilities of the different management levels as well as different participants.

Last, there is public concern about ways of providing equal opportunities to access education under the context of class polarization caused by the development of a market economy.

The above issues need urgent solutions if ET is to meet demands of national development in the near future.

CONDITIONS FOR FURTHER DEVELOPMENT OF ET IN VIETNAM

Based on the achievements as well as limitations still besetting ET, certain conditions for further development in Vietnam in terms of policy, legislation, socioeconomic environment and investment have been created.

Policy

Appropriate policy can be considered as the most vital factor deciding the accomplishment of the desired ends of ET.

As mentioned above, the substantive policy approved by the 6th, and reaffirmed by the 7th, Congress of Vietnam Communist Party regarding ET as the first national priority and a basic condition ensuring socioeconomic development, has in fact become a source of new understanding about the place and role of ET. ET has been redefined as a factor defining the continuing rise, or the failure, of the country. Thus, on the one hand this means that investment in ET is investment for national development and must be given priority. But, on the other hand, ET is then the responsibility of the whole of society. In its turn, ET should be based on and satisfy diversified demands of socioeconomic development, including the ensuring of social equality as the essence of socialist-orientated development in Vietnam.

This new approach has become a platform for major policies related to ET, such as diversifying ET, socialization of ET, expanding resource bases of ET, and the restructuring of ET systems. These policies have become a basis for orientation of further developments of ET.

Legislation

Some major policies have been authorized through legislation, regulations and directives. Some of these are for example, the 1992 Constitution of the Social Republic of

Vietnam, Article 35, which defines ET as the first national priority policy; the Law on Universalizing Primary Education enacted by the National Assembly in August 1991; Decision No. 241 issued by the Prime Minister on introducing tuition fees; Decree No. 90/CP issued by the government of Vietnam on the structure of the educational system and the system of certificates, diplomas and degrees awarded at different educational levels, and so on.

The issue of legislation requires special attention as the shortage of relevant legislation documentations is a serious obstacle to translating policies into action, thus leading to less effective management.

Socio-Economic Environment

An important factor having a strong influence on the implementation of ET development policies is a favourable social environment.

First and foremost, this is the strong commitment of both the government and the people to ET, which has been witnessed even at the most critical moments of history. This is the very commitment that helps ET not only to be maintained, but also to develop and to keep abreast of the nation's development. Other healthy element of the social environment are the traditional beliefs and attitudes of the people about the benefits and values that ET may bring to individuals as well as the whole of society. This social environment may be a valuable factor for ET development, if there are appropriate policies involving all participants and encouraging their contribution to ET development.

The stabilization and initial growth of Vietnam's economy under the market mechanism may also be considered as a basic condition ensuring the continuing development of ET. Since 1992, annual GDP growth has increased by over 8 per cent and considerable progress has been made in such major economic fields as agriculture, light industry and services, attracting more domestic and foreign investment.

This stable and progressive development of Vietnam's economy is closely interlinked with the development of ET. On the one hand, this poses new challenges for ET to meet: namely, that ET should be one step in advance, to prepare proper human resources for developing the market economy. On the other hand, stable economic growth has always been a solid ground for ET development. However, there is an increasing gap between the rich and low income groups as a negative consequence of the growing market economy. This matter requires serious consideration in the setting up of development plans for education.

Investment

Even though ET is thought of as the first national priority, so far its development has not been offered investment priority. The state budget allocated for ET is still limited, only slightly increasing from 8 per cent in 1990 to 10.56 per cent in 1995. A part of the total budget of ET is covered by local budgets.

Certain policies have been implemented in order to mobilize investment in ET from other non-state sources. These policies include the introducing of tuition fees, the encouragement of income-generating activities by educational institutions, the facilitation of the establishment of privately-founded institutions and schools, and mobilizing foreign investment by grants and loans.

It is also worthy of note that improvement in international co-operation with other countries in the region and the world has created for Vietnam's ET not only an opportunity to attract assistance, but also to participate in the international progressive trends of education.

ORIENTATIONS FOR ET DEVELOPMENT UP TO 2020

In the coming decades, Vietnam aims to achieve strong growth in its economic development, to build up a developed, equal and civilized society on a basis of promoting industrialization and modernization of the country.

These ambitious goals cannot be achieved without highly developed human resources, which are critical to national development. Thus, there are new challenges for ET – the producer of required human resources. Under the new circumstances, the general objective of ET up to 2020 is to improve both quality and quantity of ET to the level of regional and international standards, to provide human resources necessary for industrialization and modernization of the country, and to maintain its position in co-operation and competition with other countries.

The system of ET in Vietnam at the beginning of the twenty-first century should have these desired characteristics:

● A system of basic education aimed at the improvement of the educational level of the whole population;
● A system effectively providing necessary manpower for socioeconomic developments;
● A system with a priority to provide excellent ET (to develop talent and train highly qualified specialists);
● A system capable of attracting investment from the government, employers and clients; and
● A system integrated with ET in the rest of the world.

Some target numbers are determined as below.

Improving Education Level of the Whole Population

Until the year 2010, the target is: to increase the literacy rate from 89 per cent to 97 per cent; and to 99 per cent by the year of 2020; to complete the universalization of primary education; to raise that lower-secondary attendance rate from 50 per cent in 1995 to 80 per cent in the year 2010, and 90 per cent in 2020; and the post-secondary attendance rate from 5 per cent in 1995 to 20 per cent in 2010 and 25 per cent in 2020.

Training Manpower

To increase the rate of professionally orientated school students to 10 per cent in 2000 and 25 per cent in 2010; the rate of the qualified workforce from 12 per cent in 1995 to 25 per cent in 2000 and 50 percent in 2010; and the number of university graduates per 1000 population from 11 in 1995 to 15 in 2000 and to 25 in 2010.

Fostering Talent

Centres of excellence are to be established, where in teaching programmes, methods and facilities reach international standards. The number of students attending these centres is to be increased progressively from 5 per cent at the time of writing to 10 per cent by the year 2000 and 20 per cent in 2010. This will build some higher education units up to the international level of research and training, to expand opportunities for Vietnamese people to obtain and to upgrade qualifications and experience education overseas.

As can be seen above, the goals are very ambitious. How can ET achieve international standards, ensure its quality, and effectively meet increasing demands of the dynamic socioeconomic development when resources given to solving these tasks are still very limited.

Critical to a successful implementation of the policy is a system of feasible and relevant measures. Some of them are considered below.

- Improving the structure of the educational system by diversifying it to different branches: education for all (eradicating illiteracy, improving the educational level of the population); education of excellent quality (developing talents, training highly-qualified manpower); and education for the needs of particular geographical areas, economic zones and economic fields.
- Reorganizing the network of ET institutions: restructuring higher education institutions into national

multidisciplinary universities, regional universities, and community colleges; and ranking ET institutions by sources and scale of funding.

- Improving objectives, content and methods of ET at different levels by following the progressive trends in the world and closely linking these with the practice of Vietnam.
- Strengthening socialization of ET, improving management and effectiveness of non-state schools and institutions.
- Ensuring social equality by providing a minimum level of education for all people, expanding vocational education, offering loans for poor students, and giving priority to disadvantaged areas.
- Enhancing qualifications and motivation of teaching staff by standardizing and classifying them at different levels, encouraging their professional development, and improving their living conditions.
- Expanding funding for ET by increasing the state budget allocation from 11 per cent in 1995 to 15 per cent in 2000, and 17–20 per cent in 2010; mobilizing contributions from employers, communities, clients, and social organizations; and encouraging foreign investment by grants and loans.
- Upgrading infrastructure, teaching and learning facilities, especially for centres of excellence.
- Improving educational management by promoting legislation, defining responsibilities at different management level, establishing Education Management Information System (EMIS) to serve management and development of ET.
- Strengthening international co-operation by exchanging information, publications, staff and students; implementing effective co-operation projects and programmes; improving the efficiency of utilization of foreign grants and loans; and encouraging intellectual and material contributions from Vietnamese living overseas.

INTERNATIONAL CO-OPERATION AND INVESTMENT

Co-operation and investment are considered to be two important measures to bring about the strategy of ET in Vietnam.

Prior to 1990, the key donors were East European countries. Under the framework of grant aid signed by the Vietnamese government with the governments of these countries, thousands of people obtained and upgraded their qualifications overseas. Assistance was given also by providing equipment, books, and materials for ET institutions in Vietnam. It is fair to say that, given the difficulties and limitations facing Vietnam through its various wars over a forty-year period, the above assistance contributed very significantly to ET development in Vietnam. Thanks to such assistance, a considerable contingent of specialists was established.

After 1990, with the changes in the former socialist countries, such assistance given to Vietnam has become more limited. In its place with the adoption of an 'open policy' and the lifting of the US-imposed embargo on Vietnam, opportunities for investment and co-operation in ET have been expanded progressively through grants and loans.

The major bilateral donors in the ET sector are listed in the Report by the Government of Vietnam to the 'Sectoral Aid Co-ordination Meeting on Education', as follows :

Australia	Graduate training and establishment of English language centres (US$12.5 million).
Japan	Upgrading Can Tho University and supporting primary schools affected by typhoons (US$2.7 million).
Sweden	Assistance to the Economic Management Training Centre and Training Course at Master level in Economics (US$2.7 million).
Switzerland	Assistance to the Forestry College and vocational training centres (US$3.2 million).

Germany	Assistance to vocational teacher training schools (US$12 million).
France	Assistance to the French-Vietnamese Centre, training banking and economic personnel.
Thailand	Upgrading of BacThai Agriculture College. Assistance to Tu Liem Vocational Training Centre.
South Korea	Assistance in renovating two vocational training schools.

Assistance is also provided by various international organisations such as United Nations Development (UNDP) with a total aid grant of US$10 million for nine projects; United Nations Children Fund (UNICEF): US$7 million for six projects, and United Nations Population Fund (UNFPA): US$3.5 million for five projects.

Concessional loans are given by some financial institutions for some major projects. These include US$70 million loans from the World Bank for implementation of the Primary Education Project during 1994–2001, US$40 million loans from the Asian Develoment Bank (ADB) for the Secondary Education Project; and requests for loans of US$60 million are being considered by the World Bank for the Project of Higher Education Reform and Consolidation.

The intensive development of ET, as mentioned above, requires very large funding: for upgrading infrastructure, improving teaching and learning facilities, developing curriculum, and enhancing the capacity of teaching staff. Given limited domestic resources, assistance from outside may be of very great help. As an estimation made in the Report by the government to the 'Sectoral Aid Coordination Meeting on Education' shows, for the period 1996–2000, investment in education needs about VN$125 000 billion 100 000 billion of which may be mobilized from the sources within Vietnam while the rest – VN$25 000 billion (or US$2.5 billion) needs to be mobilized from other sources and official development assistance (ODA).

However, investments from foreign sources can be of great significance only if they are used effectively in the proper priority areas. These priority programmes and projects for the development of ET are identified in the Report by the government to the 'Sectoral Aid Coordination Meeting on Education', as follows:

- Improving quality in general education;
- Rehabilitation and expansion of the school infrastructure for primary and lower-secondary;
- Strengthening and diversifying non-formal education;
- Making vocational training more relevant to labour market needs;
- Rationalizing, upgrading and strengthening higher education; and
- Strengthening educational management.

VIETNAMESE–AUSTRALIAN CO-OPERATION IN EDUCATION

Since 1991, Australia has become one of the largest donors, with assistance being focused mainly on training. Under the framework of Australia Aid (which used to be AIDAB, and is now AusAID), since 1993, a large number of fellowships for Vietnamese students have been provided (154 in 1993, 216 in 1994, and 250 in 1995). Besides this, short-term courses are provided under the framework of projects for scientific, technical and managerial staff. The training of pilots for Vietnam (US$6 million) continues.

Vietnamese–Australian co-operation is carried out also through various other activities such as exchange schemes, participation in professional conferences, workshops, and study tours, and invitations to experts to contribute to courses organized in Vietnam.

It can be said that, given the changes taking place in Vietnam's ET, assistance programme from Australia represents an important opportunity for a number of Vietnamese students and staff to communicate with

Western theories and practices, and to improve their competence in various disciplines. However, this assistance may bring more efficiency if it is not scattered and fragmented but is focused on training, and formulating contingents of highly qualified staff capable of speeding up the development in some priority areas, especially in those areas important to Vietnam. Some of these areas are agriculture, economics, management, education and social sciences. Furthermore, it would be more effective if the assistance from the Australian side was co-ordinated on a nationwide scale.

Bibliography

Dang Ba Lam, 'Human Resources Development Vietnam.' *Development Papers No. 16*, UNESCAP (in English).

Draft Report on Strategic Orientations of Education and Training Development up to 2020, Ministry of Education and Training, Hanoi, 1996 (in Vietnamese).

Ministry of Educational Training. 50 Years of Education and Training Development (1945–1995), Publishing House 'GD', 1995 (in Vietnamese).

Report by the Government of Vietnam to 'Sectoral Aid Co-ordination Meeting on Education', Hanoi, 1995 (in Vietnamese and English).

Resolution of the 4th Plenum of Central Committee of Communist Party Vietnam (1991) (in Vietnamese).

Tran Hong Quan, 'Objectives, Directions and Measures of Education and Training up to 2020', *Education Review*, No. 2 (1996) (in Vietnamese).

5 Vietnam's Energy Industry and Its Prospects

Nguyen Van Thach

GENERAL BACKGROUND

After ten years of implementing a renovation and open-door policy, the Vietnamese economy has notched up encouraging achievements. The average GDP was 8.5 per cent in the 1991–4 period, 8 per cent in 1995 and 9.5 per cent in 1995. The inflationary rate reduced considerably from 500 per cent to 68 per cent in 1991, 17.5 per cent in 1992, and 14.4 per cent in 1994.

In parallel with the high economic growth rate, Vietnam's energy industry has made remarkable progress. Crude oil output increased from 40 000 tonnes in 1976 to 7 616 000 tonnes in 1995; coal output went up from 4.6 million tonnes in 1990 to 5.9 million tonnes in 1995; and electricity output climbed from 8790 million kW in 1990 to 12 473 million kW in 1994. The average growth rates of crude oil, coal and electricity were 35.9 per cent, 3.8 per cent, and 9.5 per cent, respectively, in the 1989–94 period (see Table 5.1).

This growth rate of industry can be attributed to the transformation from a centrally planned economy into a market one. The opening of the economy has brought about a number of good results, boosting national industrialization in a favourable way. However, despite the considerable developments recorded by Vietnam's energy industry, it cannot completely satisfy the requirement of industrialization. Electricity output per capita in Vietnam was only 168.1 kWh in 1994, coal output per capita,

Table 5.1 Major production in Vietnam

Order	Index	Unit	1976	1985	1989	1993	Growth 1975–85	Growth 1985–89	Growth 1989–93
1	GDP	VND billion	207 962	310 390	381 500	–	4.6	5.3	–
		At 1989 prices	–	–	–	36 735	–	–	7.6
2	Food and food stuffs production	million tonnes	13.5	18.2	21.5	26.0	3.4	4.3	3.9
3	Coal production	million tonnes	5.70	5.70	5.10	6.15	0.0	Reduced	3.8
4	Power production	GW	3 089	4 230	7 792	12 269	3.6	16.5	9.5
5	Crude oil production	1000 tonnes	–	–	1 490	6 900	–	–	35.9
6	Food and foodstuffs production	Kg/capita/year	275.0	304.0	334.0	356.2	1.1	2,4	1.3
7	Coal production	Kg/capita/year	115.9	93.9	92.8	87.3	Reduced	Reduced	Reduced
8	Electricity production	Kg/capita/ year	62.8	87.2	117.1	168.1	3.7	7.6	7.5
9	Crude oil production	Kwh/capita/year	–	–	42.0	105.5	–	–	20.2

Sources: The General Statistical Department, Hanoi, various reports.
Institute for Energy, Hanoi, various reports.
Data for 1994: it is estimated that the Vietnamese population in 1994 was 72.996m.

87.3 kg; and crude oil output per capita, 105.5 kg. The supply capacity per capita of commercialized rudimentary forms of energy in Vietnam was low according to global standards: 0.093 t.o.e. in 1989 and 0.120 t.o.e. in 1993.

OVERVIEW OF ENERGY SUPPLY–DEMAND IN VIETNAM

According to the estimates of the supply capability of primary energy products to satisfy the local demand (excluding exports), the growth rate of Vietnam's energy industry was 7.6 per cent in the 1985–94 period:

- *Coal* Average output before 1985 was 5.6 million tonnes per year, which reduced to 5.1 million tonnes per year in the 1985–94 period. From 1989, local coal consumption was dampened by 1 million tonnes per year compared with previous years. However, things have changed for the better since 1995.
- *Hydropower* Because of success in the exploitation of hydropower sources, electricity output recorded a leap of six times as much as previous years, with a growth rate averaging 21.5 per cent annually in the 1985–94 period.
- *Crude oil* The growth rate was very high in the 1989–94 period, averaging 35.7 per cent per year. Output of crude oil was 1.5 million tonnes, 2.7 million tonnes, 4.0 million tonnes, 5.5 million tonnes, 6.3 million tonnes and 6.9 million tonnes in 1989, 1990, 1991, 1992, 1993 and 1994, respectively.

Energy Imports

Excluding a small amount of imported coal, the main energy imports of Vietnam before 1995 were diesel oil (DO), fuel oil (FO), aviation fuel, kerosene and lubricants, because Vietnam's oil refining and petrochemical industry was only slowly developing at that time. In 1993, energy products accounted for the biggest proportion of total imports, being 83.4 per cent, including mainly raw materials (72.1 per cent), machinery (19.2 per cent), and oil exploiting equipment (8.7 per cent).

Despite the rapid development of hydropower plants that has helped reduce the consumption level of DO and FO in diesel power and oil thermal power production, extensive growth in the means of transport has led to a soaring importation of oil products, the consumption growth of which increased from an average of 10.4 per cent before 1989 to 13.4 per cent in the 1989–94 period. However, according to forecasts by experts, in the coming years there will be a high demand for imported electricity because of the level of electricity loss, while being decreased, is still high compared with that in other regional countries. In 1994, the power loss rate was 21.8 per cent at Electricity Company Number 1; 18.7 per cent at Electricity Company Number 2; and 23.5 per cent at Electricity Company Number 3. The total loss over the whole industry was 22.52 per cent.

According to the 1995 plan, the power losses should be 18.04 per cent, 19.8 per cent and 22.0 per cent at Electricity Company Numbers 1, 2 and 3, respectively. The economic and technical standards for the production of 1 kWh in Vietnam are still very backward. For example, coal thermal power; 4140 kcal/kWh (while advanced countries' average level is 2500 kcal/kWh); single-cycle oil air-turbine; 3764 kcal/kWh (comprehensive air-turbine; 2000 kcal/kWh); oil thermal power, 2812 kcal/kWh (air thermal power; 2250 kcal/kWh). With the existing and expanding electricity sources, it was forecast that by 1997, Vietnam would suffer a loss of about 250 mvV, which would result in a shortage of electricity from February until May in the South of Vietnam annually, leading to a quickly increasing load in this area. This forecast was been found to be conservative.

Energy Exports

Before 1995, the two main kinds of exported energy from Vietnam were crude oil and coal. With coal exports, because of a degrading infrastructure in coal exploitation and unfavourable changes in the global coal market, the exported amount is not stable. This can be shown clearly below (unit = 1000 tonnes; numbers are rounded up):

1990	740
1991	945
1992	1305
1993	1735
1994	2005

The Vietnam General Corporation of Coal had planned to satisfy both the local consumption and export demands in 1996 and 1997. More specifically, in 1996, the local exports were US$99 million, equal to 125 per cent of the annual plan, increasing by 44 per cent over the previous year; in 1997, the turnover reached US$102 million, going up by 3 per cent over the year 1996. In addition, the Corporation will try to maintain an exported volume of no less than 3 million tonnes per year. This is a long-term target in the 1996–2000 plan of the Corporation.

As for oil, because the oil refining industry is still at an embryonic stage, most of the exploited crude oil has been sold to foreign countries. As already mentioned above, the average growth rates were 35.7 per cent and 26.4 per cent respectively in the 1989–94 and 1990–94 periods, with crude oil output for 1994 being 4.6 times as much as that of 1989.

Generally speaking, the year 1990 can be considered as a milestone, marking a balance between energy exports and imports. In that year, energy exported from and imported into Vietnam reached 202 kt.o.e., with the exported volume of crude oil and coal exceeding the imported oil products.

DEVELOPMENT ORIENTATIONS OF VIETNAM'S ENERGY INDUSTRY IN 1996–2000–2010

1. Properly exploiting the energy sources on the basis of a master plan; utilizing in an economical and

highly effective way forms and sources of rudimentary energy; reducing energy losses; and protecting the living environment in the process of energy exploitation and utilization.

2. Taking full advantage of foreign investment in the forms of joint venture, co-operation, product-sharing contracts and so on.

3. Strengthening the spearhead energy branch of oil and gas; and exploring and exploiting more strongly the oil and gas potential of Vietnam.

4. Full exploiting water sources in terms of hydropower, irrigation and transport, concentrating on three main rivers including the Da River (Son La), Sesan (Yali) and Dong Nai (where emphasis is put on middle-sized hydro power stations).

5. Developing air and coal thermal power.

6. Developing coal production, and especially coal exportation.

7. Making preparations for the exploitation of atomic electric power after the year 2010.

8. Developing in a synchronized and balanced way systems of power transmission and distribution, reducing energy losses and abuse.

9. Making an appropriate investment in the management of energy demands under the guideline of managing energy demands with high efficiency, economizing, and looking for substitutes for energy, low loss and abuse being an intensive investment for development.

10. Doing research on new forms of energy to serve daily life and socioeconomic requirements in the areas that are in a position to integrate themselves into the national energy network.

Development Plan for Vietnam's Coal Industry – Several Large Programmes

1. The technological renovation programme. Its objectives are to reduce as much as possible the earth

peeling coefficient; improve the coal quality; reduce the transportation costs to the lowest possible level; and apply feasible technological solutions in a highly efficient way in the exploitation of open-cast mines. As for underground exploitation, set targets are to improve the coal quality; increase the level of mechanization in gallery digging to prepare for the next steps; speed up the pace of digging and productivity; reduce wood consumption and coal losses; and take full advantage of exploitation technologies that allow for a high level of obtained output.

2. The synchronization and modernization programme in the 1996–2010 period:

● Making full use of the existing infrastructure, equipment and human resources. Making intensive investment, synchronizing and modernizing in combination with making new investments in small and medium-sized mines, processing, transport, and loading and unloading establishments in order to increase capacity and output, and satisfy demands for coal in terms of quantity and category at home and abroad.

● Assessing the influence on the environment and environmental protection:

(a) Establishing environment observing stations in the area of coal mines in order to supply regular information on the situation and causes of environmental and air pollution.

(b) Evaluating the effects on the environment caused by coal mines (in Cam Pha, Hon Gai and so on) so that active preventive measures can be taken in order to provide ecological and environmental protection.

(c) Strengthening the effectiveness of environmental sanitation in the coal exploitation and processing industry.

3. Informatics technology application programme:

● Building a computer network in the whole industry in order to quickly provide exact information, effectively serving the requirements of business management.

- Establishing a control system of databases concerning geology and the coal environment in order to strengthen the management of natural resources and the environment.
- Applying informatics in planning, designing, technological management and production in the mining areas.

4. Multi-branch business development programme. Making full use of existing infrastructure, equipment and human resources in combination with new investment, to develop effectively non-coal business activities, create and increase the production value of non-coal activities from 23.9 per cent in 1996 to 40 per cent by the year 2000.

Development Plan for the Power Industry of Vietnam

1. The development plan for the Power industry of Vietnam includes:
   - Meeting the national demand of the economy for electricity, which will be 25–27 billion kWh and 60–65 kWh in the years 2000 and 2010, respectively. The demand for electricity in the year 2000 will be identified through the direct forecast method, and the demand for electricity in 2010 identified through the elasticity method.
   - Strengthening and completing the existing power sources and networks, well satisfying electricity demands, which will reach 25–27 billion kWh – that is, 300 kWh per capita – per year.
   - Basically completing the improvement of power networks in such large cities as Hanoi, Hai Phong, Nam Dinh, Hue, Qui Nhon and so on. Transmitting power from the national network to 80 per cent of the villages nationwide, and the remaining 20 per cent being supplied by electricity from small hydro power stations, diesel, wind or

solar energy, or other new forms of energy under research after the year 2000.

• Reducing electricity losses to 0.5–1 per cent per year, working out measures against power pilferage and abuse in daily life.

• Finding out immediate measures to overcome the shortage of electricity.

• Through appropriate measures in management of production and capital construction, and thoroughly practising thrift in the use of investment capital, production costs, reducing electricity losses and other costs to a minimum to decrease production costs, reduce losses and gain profits.

Development Plan for the Oil and Gas Industry

1. Extending forms of investment and co-operation to develop the industry.
2. Accelerating the construction and completion of an oil refining industrial area to satisfy the fast increasing demand for oil at home, especially in the field of transportation.

VIETNAM'S ENERGY INDUSTRY – PROSPECTS FOR FOREIGN INVESTMENT

For the Coal Market

Coal is not a renewable natural resource. Exploitation conditions are increasingly difficult, with bigger risks; construction and capacity stabilization periods last for a long time (5–7 years); and most production materials must be imported while the domestic price set to serve local consumption in low. Therefore, the demand for capital and coal development technology is very high, especially in a situation where the infrastructure is still very poor, but the coal industry cannot have its own capital source for development. Priority will be given to the synchronization of production lines, the evaluation and selection phases, ports, transportation, production of substitutes and the transferral of modern technologies.

What should be emphasized now is to make extensive investment and expand new mines as well as to make intensive investment in the mines through technological improvement, the synchronization of equipment and increases in exploitation capacity. According to the development plan for the coal industry up to the year 2000, there should be an investment capital amount of about 600 billion VN$, of which the energy credit capital and capital depreciation only account for 50 per cent; the remaining 50 per cent will be mobilized from foreign countries. Currently, main sources of finance for the industry come from Japanese trade companies.

For Electric Power

The investment capital for the electric power industry in the five-year plan from 1996–2000 is VN$5700 billion, half of which is foreign capital with an annual investment level doubling that of the five-year plan from 1991 to 1995. Because of an insignificant amount of electricity energy exports and a large volume of imported electricity production equipment, it is the state that has to borrow from foreign countries. Previously, in the 1980–90 period, when the subsidized economy still existed, an unreasonable allocation in the investment capital structure led to low investment effectiveness in the power industry. Therefore the state has now issued policies concerning the renovation of the industry in a long-term orientation of commercialization, equitization and privatization, of which commercialization has a very great advantage in calling for foreign investment and looking for partners.

In the coming years, the borrowing of capital from official development assistance (ODA) sources is estimated at VN$22 000 billion and investment capital in the form of build–operate–transfer (BOT), VN$12 000 billion.

Investment capital from other sources (for example, domestic loans, commercial loans, capital depreciation and so on) is forecast to be VN$23 000 billion.

In the 1996–2000 period, various forms of investment such as joint ventures, BOT, BOOT (build–operate–operate–transfer), and IPP (independent power plants) will be developed, among which BOT and BOOT will account for a relatively large share in the investment structure, being estimated at 38.5 per cent of total investment in the whole industry. Many investment projects in the forms of BOT and BOOT have obtained considerable success in some countries, such as India, China, Laos and Thailand. In Vietnam, under the present situation, BOT and BOOT should be applied first to low-quality coal thermal power plants and hydro power stations, which are now at a big advantage and attracting foreign investors, thanks to a domestically available source of fuel, a not very great demand for capital, and increased speed of obtaining profits.

In addition, also included in the projected development for the 1996–2000–2010 period is an important issue: the investment policy on energy development in rural and mountainous areas, with two large programmes, including:

1. Investment in the acceleration of electrification in rural areas in the 1995–2010 period, with an investment capital amount being estimated at about VN$35 000 billion, equal to US$3 billion.
2. Investment in developing various forms of energy for use in daily life in rural and mountainous areas, in order to stop the utilization of the traditional fuel, trees. Investment projects in energy development in rural areas should be evaluated in terms of ecological character, practice, customs, religions, average income, local character and the traditional energy self-supply structure in those areas, to ensure that even those with the lowest incomes can still enjoy energy consumption at a minimum level.

For Oil and Gas

1. On the basis of the officially issued Law on Foreign Investment in 1987, calling for foreign investment in this field in the form of multilateral co-operation, product-sharing contracts or bidding and so on.
2. Extending forms of co-operation and investment, besides the joint ventures such as Vietsopetro, boosting up the signing of product-sharing contracts whereby the value of the Vietnamese side should gradually be increased. Quickly completing the establishment of a petrochemical and refining industry to satisfy domestic increasing demands without any prejudice to the output of exported crude oil.

In the future, oil and gas will be a spearhead energy industry in Vietnam. With a lot of latent potential on the move to be developed rapidly, investment effectiveness in this field will be very satisfactory.

Investment Prospects for Australia

It can be seen that trade relations between Vietnam and Australia have achieved noticeable steps forward in the recent years. Australia is a trade partner of Vietnam in many fields, with increasing investment in Vietnam showing the country is becoming a promising market.

In the energy industry, Australia has retained a considerable export–import relationship with Vietnam. The main import from Australia to serve the industry of Vietnam is crude oil. In the future, when Vietnam's energy industry further develops, Australia will have an extremely important role in supporting this development process with capital, human resources, and especially technological transfer and highly feasible investment projects in the forms of BOT and BOOT and so on, as mentioned above. Australia has established a firm foothold in the Vietnamese market with the presence of such large firms as Telstra (in the telecommunications field) and BHP (in oil and gas exploitation). It is hoped that in the near future, the bilateral trade relations between the two countries will be further promoted, strengthened and multilaterally developed.

6 Banking and Financial Operations in Vietnam

ICTC staff

GENERAL BACKGROUND

From the end of the 1970s, before the 6th National Congress, Vietnam began grappling with a socioeconomic crisis in which production slipped into stagnation and loss-making. In the period 1976–81, the annual production growth rate was 0.4 per cent, the population grew at a rate of 2.3–2.4 per cent per year, inflation increased uncontrollably, external economic relations were stagnant, the country was still subject to blockade and embargo, and living standards declined sharply. As a result, the economy was in serious crisis, which peaked when hyperinflation reached 774.7 per cent in 1986.

Since the 6th National Congress, Vietnam has adopted the 'Doi Moi' (renovation) process in the economy. The Vietnamese government, while managing to maintain political stability, has, step by step, resolved its urgent socioeconomic problems. Hyperinflation has been controlled, from the triple-digit rate (393.8 per cent in 1988) to a mere double-digit rate in the mid-1990s. The industrial growth rate in the period 1991–5 was 13.3 per cent, compared to the late 1980s when it was 5.9 per cent. Import–export has gradually increased, the ratio of imports to exports in particular being improved. Capital accumulation from within the economy has begun. Investment by the whole of society in capital construction was 15.8 per cent of GDP in 1990, and 27.4 per cent in 1994 (of which domestic capital amounted to 16.7 per cent of GDP). By the end of 1995, total registered foreign invested capital had reached about US$18 billion, with a third already put into operation (see Figures 6.1–6.5).

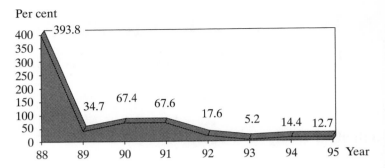

Figure 6.1   Inflation (per cent)

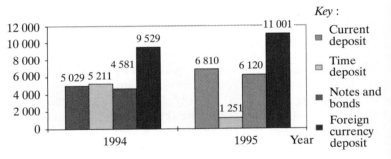

Figure 6.2   Capital mobilized from domestic sources

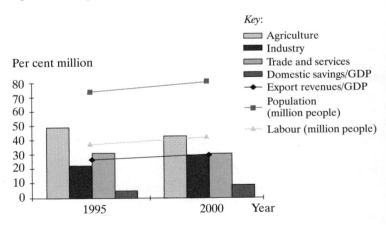

Figure 6.3   Key economic indicators in Vietnam, 1995–2000

(a) Investment
   per project

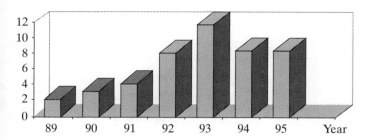

(b) Investment capital in
    1989–95

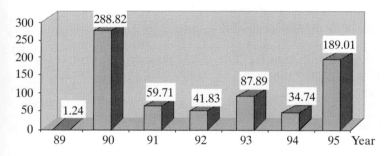

(c) Capital per investment area

Per cent

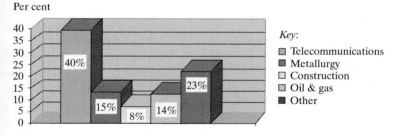

Figure 6.4 Statistical data relating to Australian investment in Vietnam

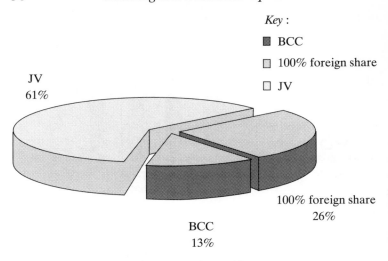

Figure 6.5   Number of projects per form of investment

Under the general 'Doi Moi' process, certain remarkable achievements in the areas of banking and finance have been obtained and helped to make changes in the process of developing the country's economy and sustaining political stability.

BANKING AND FINANCIAL OPERATIONS

With respect to the state budget, Vietnam has successfully met all objectives specified in its long-term plan for 1990–5. In this period, the state budget has changed from a situation in which revenues from domestic sources were not sufficient to meet current expenditure, to a situation in which revenues from domestic sources are sufficient to meet current expenditure and payments of foreign loans, and to set aside part of them for development investment. Wholly-subsidized schemes applicable to state-owned enterprises have been removed. The budget deficit is controllable, and gradually decreasing. Sources to cover state budget deficits have changed. In past years, these sources were mainly bonds and commercial loans, but they are now in the form of loans raised from the public and from favourable foreign sources. The tax system has been reformed, and the collectable amount of taxes and fees has doubled in comparison with 1990.

Adherence to stabilization and reform policies provided a basis for official creditors to make loans totalling about US$0.6 billion in 1996. Of which, US$175 million were from the International Monetary Fund (IMF) under the three-year Enhanced Structural Adjustment Facility (ESAF). Drawdowns in current and prospective lending programmes of the World Bank's International Development Association (IDA) and the Asian Development Bank (ADB) raised the net flows of multilateral creditors gradually from close to US$0.1 billion in 1994 to almost US$0.3 billion in 1996. Persistent project delays are likely to limit the utilization of large commitments of government-to-government credits. However, net flows from official bilateral creditors reached around US$0.2 billion in 1996.

The role of foreign banks in the foreseeable future will be influenced by the resolution of arrears in medium-term loans. In the short term, foreign banks may only extend small loans to Vietnam. Limits on new commercial borrowing imposed by the IMF's ESAF will, however, restrain additional medium-term borrowing. Borrowings from non-banking private creditors may reach US$0.1 billion annually. Payments to such creditors are hindered by difficulties, although Vietnam and the group of foreign suppliers agreed in 1994 to defer payments for these loans.

Total external debts in convertible foreign reached US$6 billion in 1996 from US$4.7 billion at the end of 1994. The Paris Club agreement has reduced total interest payments due from more than US$0.3 billion in 1992 to US$0.2–0.3 billion by the end of 1996. Total debt service remained at around 6 per cent of exports of goods and services in 1996.

In the insurance and auditing areas, the Vietnamese government appears to wish to keep its monopolistic position and to be reluctant to open itself to foreign investors. However, under the forces of the market economy it is encouraging to develop, the government has adopted participation therein by foreign investors, with a number of restrictions. At the time of writing, a number of newly-established insurance and auditing joint ventures exist. These joint ventures have promoted the competition and efficiency of domestic companies and forced them to reform.

With respect to the banking area, Vietnam has enacted two fundamental ordinances: the first is the Ordinance on the State Bank and the other is the Ordinance on Banks, Credit Co-operatives and Financial Companies. A remarkable result the ordinances have had has been the creation of a two-echelon banking system. After a five-year implementation of the two ordinances, the economic structure of the sectors in the banking system has changed. By 31 December 1995, in addition to four state-owned commercial banks, there were forty-eight joint stock commercial banks, nineteen foreign bank branches and four joint venture banks. Additionally, there were 182 people's credit funds. At the time of writing, there are seventy-five banks in Vietnam (excluding people's credit funds) with total assets accounting for VN$46 912 billion (around US$4500 million).

Besides domestic banks, foreign banks in the form of foreign bank branches operating in Vietnam have appeared. These branches have played an important role in the mobilization of foreign loans to Vietnam, and the creation of standard criteria for modernizing the banking technology for domestic banks. With only a simple personnel organization, these branches have had a trading turnover bigger than that of domestic joint-stock commercial banks. In the late 1990s, total capital mobilized by these banks has reached VN$5000 billion. Capital raised from organizations and individuals is increasing steadily, accounting for 50 per cent of total deposits in 1995, from only 20 per cent in 1993. Total loans made by the banks reached VN$6894 billion at the end of 1995, of which, 32.4 per cent was extended to the public sector, 23.6 per cent to the foreign invested sector, 21.3 per cent to the non-public sector, and 17 per cent to Vietnamese banks. Of the first foreign banks, Crédit Lyonnais, ANZ and Chinfon are able to provide diversifying banking services.

According to estimates by policy planners, in order to double the country's per capital income to US$400 per annum by the year 2000, Vietnam needs US$42 billion, of which US$13–14 billion will be raised from foreign direct investment, US$7–8 billion from ODA sources, and an ambitious US$21 billion from domestic sources. However, sustainability of these capital flows is being threatened, particularly for the domestic target.

FUNDAMENTAL LEGAL DOCUMENTS ON BANKING AND FINANCE

In 1995, the Vietnamese National Assembly enacted the Budget Law, which became the first-ever law in Vietnam regulating this area. The law provides for the preparation, implementation, balance and inspection of state budgets and rights and responsibilities of state agencies at all levels in the state budget area. The government and its relevant ministries are drafting documents guiding the implementation of this law.

A foreign investor doing business in Vietnam may be subject to the following taxes: turnover tax under the Law on Turnover Tax; profit tax under the Law on Foreign Investment in Vietnam (LFI); withholding tax under the LFI; special sales tax under the special sales tax law (passed by Congress and amended later); royalties under the law on mineral resources; housing and land taxes under the ordinance on housing and land taxes; and other taxes and fees. Vietnam has recently stopped imposing turnover tax on banking operations in order to lower the interest rates on bank loans, and thus pump more capital into the economy.

As mentioned above, there are two ordinances regulating the banking system, both issued in 1990. One provides rights, responsibilities and structural organization of the

State Bank (Ordinance on Banks), and the other regulates banks, credit co-operatives and financial companies. A law on the State Bank and a law on banks and financial institutions are being drafted to replace the two ordinances. Foreign bank branches, however, are additionally subject to separate governmental documents. Those documents are Decree No. 189/CP of 15 June 1991 of the government on Foreign Bank Branches and Joint Venture Banks, and a number of State Bank Circulars, including Circular No. 178 dated 5 October 1991, Circular No. 06 dated 11 April 1992, Decision No. 200 dated 23 September 1992, Decision No. 188 dated 2 October 1993, and other related documents which provide guidelines on the implementation of the Ordinance on Banks and Decree No. 189. Borrowings from foreign sources are subject to Decree No. 58/CP dated 30 August 1993 of the government, and Circular No. 7 of the State Bank of Vietnam dated 26 March 1994.

Presently, insurance business is operating under Decree No. 100 on Insurance Business dated 30 May 1993. There are two circulars issued by the Ministry of Finance guiding the implementation of Decree No. 100, which are Circular No. 45 and Circular No. 46. Although the documents recognize the rights of foreign investors to establish foreign insurance company branches or new insurance joint ventures with Vietnamese parties, these rights are constrained by a number of conditions set by the government. However, so far there are two insurance joint venture companies licensed to operate in Vietnam and a number of proposals on the way for investment licenses. Auditing business is a new area in Vietnam.

PROSPECTS AND IMPLEMENTATION PROGRAMMES

Prospects

The year 1995 marked an important event in the friendly relationship between Vietnam and Australia by exchange visits to the countries by the Vietnamese General Secretary of the Communist Party, Do Muoi, and the Australian Prime Minister, Paul Keating, accompanied by a number of high-ranking officials of the two countries. This event generated goodwill towards economic co-operative relationships between the two countries.

There are now over a hundred Australian companies doing business in Vietnam. Certain informal Australian business groups have been set up in Vietnam. These groups, in the foreseeable future, will develop into a full Australian Chamber of Commerce in Vietnam. The annual bilateral trade flow between Vietnam and Australia in 1996 stood at around US$450 million, with enormous potential for growth in the future. Australia is now the eighth-largest foreign investor in Vietnam. Among Australian companies active in Vietnam, BHP and Telstra are ranked as the biggest private investors. The development assistance programme for Vietnam over the period 1995–8 drawn up by the Australian government has an expected value of $A200 million. The Australian-funded bridge at My Thuan in the Mekong delta is Australia's single largest aid project ever. The bridge cost $A73 million (US$55 million), and was designed by Maunsell, an Australian-based company. Australia is now one the largest providers of government scholarships for Vietnamese students and officials to study overseas.

An air services agreement was finalized by the two countries in March 1995. As a result, the number of direct scheduled flights between Vietnam and Australia will be likely to increase over the next few years. The number of Australians visiting Vietnam in 1995 was estimated at around 50 000 and this figure could double in 1998.

Additionally, a 180 000-strong Vietnamese community in Australia, a highest percentage of Vietnamese overseas per capita in comparison with that of any other country, will be an important source of investment into Vietnam.

Vietnam and Australia entered into a Treaty on Avoidance of Double Taxation on 13 April 1992, effective in Australia and Vietnam from 1 January 1993 and 1 July

1993, respectively. In July 1995, Vietnam was admitted as a full member of the Association of the South East Asian Nations (ASEAN), with which Australia has formal dialogue partners. It means that the participation in the ASEAN by Vietnam in turn may help Australia's direct relationship with Vietnam, and that, if Vietnam liberalizes its trading relations with ASEAN countries, Australia can take advantage of this.

The current steady development of the Vietnamese economy, the poor conditions of its infrastructure, an insufficient capability of domestic sources, and the broadening of economic co-operative relationships and so on with other countries means that Vietnam will be badly in need of capital, technology and management expertise, that must be partly imported from foreign countries. It appears that Australia, with its firm bases for doing business in Vietnam as discussed above, will have many opportunities of doing business in general, and carrying out banking and financial operations in particular.

Implementation Programmes

Strategies

In order to develop the provision of banking and financial services in Vietnam now as well as in the future, the Australian government and the companies themselves must develop the right strategies, since there is serious competition between foreign and Vietnamese companies. Such strategies will involve the following: (i) maintenance and broadening of Australia's aid programmes for Vietnam; (ii) promotion of Australian investment in Vietnam; (iii) promotion of bilateral trade flows between the two countries; and (iv) preparation to participate in a stock market in Vietnam when it is established.

Implementation Programmes

Australia's maintenance of a bilateral development assistance programme for Vietnam will not only nurture the relationships between the two countries, but also provide Australian companies with advantages for Australian companies' access to the Vietnamese market.

Generally, the Vietnamese government views personnel training as one of the top priorities in its modernization and industrialization process. Fortunately, in this field, Australia has certain advantages and is able to provide necessary expertise to Vietnam. In practice, Australia is one of the largest sponsors, providing training and education services to Vietnam. Australia is able to provide training courses about financial and capital markets to Vietnamese experts and thereby to support the establishment of capital markets, especially a stock market, in Vietnam. Australia can help Vietnam to reform its tax system, by using the self-declaration tax system, for example. In the insurance field, training insurers is one of the most important elements to enhance the development of insurance companies in Vietnam, and thus make the investment environment safer for investors. Also, Australia could assist the reform process of a treasury system in Vietnam by providing training assistance to Vietnamese trainees.

In addition to granting aid to build so-called friendship projects in Vietnam in which Australian companies have privileges to be involved, Australia should maintain its financial support by providing low-interest loans for capital construction and the development of industry in Vietnam. However, the management of such aids and loans should be restricted, to insure that such financing sources will be used in the most efficient manner.

Obviously, as the trade flow between Vietnam and Australia increases, demand for banking and financial services will increase, and this will generate more oppurtunities for Australian companies to do business in these fields.

The participation in ASEAN and the implementation of the AFTA scheme by Vietnam have made the investment environment in Vietnam more attractive to foreign investors. The reasons are low-cost labour, expansion of the consumption market, and investment incentives under the Vietnamese LFI and so on for foreign companies in general, and Australian companies in particular. This, on the other hand, will limit access to Australian-made commodities, which do not enjoy tariff incentives under AFTA. As a result, until Vietnam becomes a member of the WTO, and thus becomes subject to the rules of this, Australian companies may wish to set up production establishments in Vietnam to take up the above-mentioned advantages.

7 Vietnam's Forestry and Prospects

Pham Van Khoi

INTRODUCTION

Among the 330 363 sq.km of Vietnam's territory, 75 per cent comprises mountains and hills. Natural forests, bare hills and deserted land that has forestry potential cover roughly 200 000 sq.km, accounting for 60.5 per cent of the national area. Of the 86 310 sq.km of natural forest, production forests make up 50 000 sq.km, protective forests 28 000 sq.km, and specialized forests 6000 sq.km.

Forestry plays a pivotal role in the national economy and social life of Vietnam. However, in recent years, the forest reserve has been exploited inappropriately, and forest destruction is rising. Total forestry output only manages a slow growth, and in some years even shows a decline. In 1990, the national forestry output stood at VN$1379 billion, and in 1991 it increased to only VN$1416 billion. In 1991 and 1992, the figure fell to VN$1386 billion and VN$1371 billion, respectively. In 1995, VN$1449.4 billion was generated. The industry's output in GDP is not proportional. Annually, the logging output was reduced because new forests have yet to be planted.

Logging output in 1990 was 4 445 800 cu.m., 3 210 000 cu.m. in 1991, 2 646 600 cu.m. in 1992, and 2 884 000 cu.m. in 1993. Speciality products are exploited arbitrarily and in a scattered way, thus making management difficult. Export turnover generated from forestry products is negligible: in 1993, export value was US$49.2 million from 23 200 cu.m. of log; 40 700 cu.m. of floor plank; 283 500 cu.m. of timber; 537 tonnes of cinnamon; and 462 tonnes of anise.

For a country like Vietnam with vast forests, the contribution of forestry to the national economy is poor. Prime reasons for the situation are lack of investment, poor management, and an untrained and shrinking workforce of less than one million people.

Recently, the government has taken numerous measures to expand the industry, in particular Programme No. 327 on afforestation which began in 1993. Many forests have been closed for the purpose of restoration and new growth, and logging there is restricted.

FOREST POTENTIAL OF VIETNAM

In Vietnam, the total area of natural forests, bare hills and deserted land stands at 20 051 356 ha. In recent years, while production forests have shrunk, the forest reserve remains quite large. Production forests cover a total area of 50 000 sq.km, containing 410 million cu.m. of log and 5.5 billion bamboo trees of various kinds. Annually, 3–5 million cu.m. of log and 30 000 tonnes of firewood can be exploited. This precious reserve adequately supplies the diverse demands of production and life. The forest is also a mine of valuable specialties such as cinnamon, anise, herbal trees, and animals. More noticeably in the past few years, rubber, coffee and tea plantations have been expanded. In 1995, Vietnam exported 110 000 tonnes of rubber, 210 000 tonnes of coffee and 90 000 tonnes of cashew nuts. Export value reached US$100 million.

Production forests have a low wood reserve, averaging 34.7–90 cu.m. per hectare. Wood reserve in the protective forests is comparatively high, about 60–104 cu.m. per hectare. Tree density in the forests is rather low: 7005 trees per hectare in the densest areas, and under 4000 trees per hectare in other areas – that is, each tree is 2.5 metres from the next. According to a survey in 1993, national natural forests are valued at VN$6489.3 billion, equivalent to US$590 billion (see Table 7.1).

Table 7.1   Average wood reserve in one hectare 1993

	Wood reserve/ha	
Area	*Production forest*	*Protective forest*
1. North-west	34.7	60.0
2. North-east	35.4	65.0
3. Central	58.0	80.0
4. North of Region 4	480.0	103.0
5. Southern central coastal area	82.5	103.0
6. South-east	48.0	70.0
7. Tay Nguyen	90.0	104.0

Note: Provinces on the plain with small forest area are excluded.
Source: *Report on Natural Forests, Bare Hills and Deserted Land,*
Ministry of Forestry, Hanoi, 1993.

Vietnam has a large area of bare hills and derelict land, of about 11 million ha, that is an untapped potential. In the 1990s, the Vietnam government has introduced various incentives to develop the mountainous economy in general, and forestry in particular. Resolutions No. 327/CP and No. 733/CP, accompanied by afforestation programmes, riverbank and coastal desert land exploitation, forest farm promotion programmes and a SIDA-funded programme have mobilized a large fund for forestry development.

In 1993, Programme No. 327 planned to lend VN$584 billion, of which VN$127 billion went to 400 forestry projects, and VN$138 billion to 256 afforestation projects. In 1984, VN$540 billion was disbursed for a basic reconstruction of the industry. Investment for the industry in 1995 reached VN$450 billion. As a result, between 1991 and 1995 a new forest area of 70 000 ha was added to the existing reserve, with over two billion trees of various kinds. After ten years (1986–95), natural forests increased by 1.2 million ha, and bare hills and derelict land reduced by 2.4 million ha.

Under the industry's strategy to the year 2000, a million square metres of bare hills and derelict land will be turned into forests and agricultural land, coffee plantation areas raised from 130 000 ha to 200 000 ha, tea from 700 000 ha to 150 000 ha, rubber to 300 000 ha, and mulberry to 100 000 ha, to support 7000 tonnes of silkworms.

PROSPECTS

Vietnam has great forest potential, but because of a lack of capital and inadequate management, desired results have yet to be obtained. Under the industry's development strategies to the years 2000 and 2010, a substantial amount of capital is to be mobilized. As well as investment from the state budget and the community, foreign investment is badly needed. Recently, the field has received investment from Switzerland, Taiwan, Hong Kong and China. Up to 1999, Vietnam needs a total of US$150 million in FDI to be disbursed in forest culture and protection, training, and wood processing technology.

Australian non-governmental organizations have provided a grant of $A300 000 for forestry associations to renew technology, train forestry workers and provide related experience for Vietnamese forestry workers. Vietnam's Ministry of Forestry to be (presently the Ministry of Agriculture and Rural Development) has coordinated with Australia to carry out projects in technology improvement, reforestation, bare hill greening and afforestation in Tam Dao, Vinh Phu, Dac Lac, and the Ba Vi national park.

In the future, the demand for wood in Vietnam will be substantial. With its well-established experience in the field, Australia can provide Vietnam with capital, technology and expertise so that the volume of wood for construction and decoration will be raised, material for paper production enhanced, farm management improved, and cash crops such as rubber, coffee, tea and cotton further exploited.

8 Vietnam's Information Technology and Its Development Prospects to 2000

Nguyen Cong Hoa

L 86

~~P 39~~

P 31

GENERAL BACKGROUND

Informatics has been paid much attention and strongly developed by the Vietnamese government for a long time. From the early 1960s, groups of experts in this field were sent abroad to follow training courses. However, until the 1970s, Vietnam imported only a few computers capable of big and multi-programme generation such as ODRA, MINSK and the ES series, mainly applied in scientific, technical, educational and national defence fields, and some special-purpose electronic computers such as CELA-TRON, applied in statistical and banking branches.

In terms of computer techniques, Vietnamese informatics specialists tried to assemble some special-purpose and first-generation computers. Because of the difficulties in the transformation of the economic mechanism and the fact that the Vietnamese economy at that time had to depend a lot on foreign aid, the economic crisis lasted for a long time, and the efforts made by the state in the development of informatics technology were not successful.

Since the early 1990s, the Vietnamese economy has overcome these crises and developed a strong base of its own. The renovation and necessity for a speedy integration into the international community, economically and socially, has stimulated the development of the information technology (IT) industry in Vietnam. The application of informatics and the generalization of computers have taken large and rapid steps forward.

THE IT DEVELOPMENT IN VIETNAM

Machinery and Equipment

According to the survey carried out by the Information Technology Steering Committee under the Ministry of Science, Technology and Environment (MOSTE), the demand for the applications of IT in Vietnam is increasing, clearly showing an annual growth rate of 150 per cent in equipment supply. Calculations by the Ministry of Trade indicate that the turnover from hardware and software in Vietnam in 1995 was US$100 million and US$6 million, respectively. Industry specialists estimate that the total turnover from IT will reach US$200 million in 1998. With the present growth rate, it is forecast that, by the year 2000, the total turnover could climb to US$225 million.

Computers assembled in Vietnam are mostly personal computers. In 1995, some 70 000 units were assembled and this figure is estimated to reach 120 000 units in 1998. As a result, there will be 300 000 computers in Vietnam by the end of 1998, of which 50 per cent, originally manufactured by famous firms, account for 78 per cent of the total turnover. The rest have their origin in South East Asian companies, being assembled in Vietnam.

One noticeable thing is that there is now a shift in the business structure of the informatics industry which is shown by a higher demand for computer applications, an increasing supply of equipment concerning computer networks, multimedia and transformation of some companies' activities into the fields of system design, consulting and services. Computer software business is developing increasingly. It is estimated that, of the total turnover from IT, the turnover from personal computers manufactured by large and well-known firms accounts for 56 per cent; from multimedia, 15 per cent; and from services, 9 per cent.

In the case of US DEC, one of the three largest informatics firms in Vietnam, of the total turnover of US$5 million in 1995, personal computers account for US$3 million (60 per cent); servers account for US$1.5 million (30 per cent); consulting and services account for US$1 million (20 per cent). In the same year, 20 per cent of FPT's sales were servers.

IT INDUSTRY

It can be said that, until now, there has not been any considerable change in the development of this industry in Vietnam. Besides Japanese Fujitsu's some 100 per cent foreign-owned establishments specializing in manufacturing printed circuits for hard drives (US$78 million), there has been no large investment in this field. A number of small-scale computer assembly lines are now operational in Ho Chi Minh City, supplying approximately 60 per cent of the total assembled computers in Vietnam. According to a survey by MOSTE, Vietnam is able to install around 7000 personal computers each month.

There have been increasing numbers of joint-ventures in Vietnam to manufacture components and equipment in the communications field, the most well-known of which being the venture between Vietnam and South Korea in Hanoi that produces switchboards and optical cables; the venture between Vietnam and the Federal Republic of Germany specializing in manufacturing optical cables; co-operation with Australia to install some VIBA cable stations; and the venture with Arcatel to produce circuit boards for the E.10 switchboard which is in its initial stage and has not yet turned out any products.

In order to satisfy the requirements of economic growth, the utilization of computers and IT is increasing daily. The application of IT to the banking industry has brought about increasing practical effectiveness in recent years. In the 1991–5 period, the state invested about US$7.5 million annually in IT for the state-owned banking system (including the State Bank and four state commercial banks), which is now equipped with approximately 5000 computers. In other branches, such as Customs, Finance, the General Statistical Department and so on, the utilization of IT is considerably improved. It is estimated that the financial management information system has 3000 computers, with a total investment of US$3 million annually.

There are four large-scale information networks with e-mail services operating throughout the country, including VARNET, with 300 users; Netnam with 1000 users; Toolnet, with 200 users; and VIETnet, with 400 users. The VIETPAC national data network can supply 100 000 subscriptions for e-mail and is preparing to link with the Internet.

Computer software companies in Vietnam are very in small number, and on a small scale. One company has an average of ten staff, a total turnover of over VN$1 billion per year, but can only create a range of applied software.

Training in the Field of IT

According to the development master plan for IT, it is estimated that by the year 2000 Vietnam will need at least 20 000 experts in this field. Each year, 1500 informatics engineers are trained, and by the year 2000, Vietnam will have 6000 engineers plus 3000 university graduates annually equipped with IT knowledge. As a consequence, at present Vietnam suffers a shortage of more than 10 000 computer technicians. Since 1993, informatics has been introduced into high schools, and in the 1996–7 school year, it was introduced for the first time to primary schools (thirty primary schools in Hanoi have been chosen for this experiment).

The Development Plan for IT in Vietnam up to the Year 2000

The master plan of the National Programme on Information Technology up to the year 2000 was approved and issued by the prime minister, accompanied by Decision No. 221/TTg, on 7 April 1995. Below are the main contents of the plan, and estimations about the financial requirements for the implementation of the development plan for the IT industry in the 1996–2000 period.

Targets

The general targets of the establishment and development of IT in Vietnam up to the year 2000 have been identified by the government in Resolution No. 49/CP. The concrete targets in the development master plan for IT in the 1996–2000 period includes:

1. Establishing a system of computers and means of communications linked with each other in networks with powerful enough software, information and database systems capable of serving state management activities and key activities of the economy. Some domestic information systems should be linked with international ones.
2. Developing on a large scale the application of IT, making contributions towards improving the productivity, quality and effectiveness of production, and, step by step, modernizing important branches of production and services and National Security and Defence. Boosting the application of IT in basic investigations, exploration and exploitation of natural resources and the environment, scientific research and other activities.
3. The generalization of an 'informative culture' within society, in order to create a favourable environment for an advance towards a fully informative society.
4. Laying the foundation for an IT industry, turning out informatics products and services of high value, giving priority to the development of the 'software' industry, while at the same time making full use of the possibilities of technological transfer to develop establishments manufacturing modern computer components and informatics equipment.

In order to achieve the above-mentioned targets, to pave the way for the integration of Vietnam into the global and regional computer systems in terms of IT, the 1996–2000 master plan will focus on important programmes with the following two main contents.

Developing the Potential and Establishing the Infrastructure of IT

This content includes four important programmes projects, as follows:

1. Education and training in the field of IT. The demand for human resources for the development of IT has been clearly identified in the master plan of the National Programme on IT up to the year 2000. Vietnam will need about 20 000 experts in IT. It will also have to hold fast-track training courses to provide thousands of managers, economic and technical experts with knowledge and capacity to operate informatics equipment. This requires an education and training programme in IT to be given first priority in the coming years.

2. Research and development of IT. The basic target of the research and development of IT in Vietnam is to absorb up-to-date knowledge and have a good understanding of the development tendency of IT in the world so that programmes related to technology can be carried out in the following fields:

   - Selecting appropriate tactics of technological transfer.
   - Researching, analyzing and designing information systems in parallel with developing applied software in the state management and socioeconomic fields.
   - Researching, designing and producing IT products.

3. Development of the IT industry. This industry is a very new one in Vietnam. Therefore, the construction of this industry should be pursued actively in the

1996–2000 period and, at the same time, an effective and appropriate investment strategy should also be worked out under the guidelines of 'building the hardware industry on the basis of developing the software', so priority should be given to the development of a software industry and IT services that bring about surplus value. As for the hardware industry, possibilities of co-operation, joint ventures and technological transfer should be taken full advantage of to develop informatic equipment assembling and special-purpose communications manufacturing establishments and so on.

4. Data communications. In the recent years, a data communication branch has been established in Vietnam in parallel with the strong development of the post office and the increasing speed of informatization in the fields of banking, finance, commercial IT in state management systems. This is also to accommodate the speedy modernization of the IT infrastructure, especially in circumstances where Vietnam has to integrate itself into the international and regional community in all fields of activity. As a result, a faster development of the national data communication networks and connection with international network in some fields is required from the early years of implementing the 1996–2000 plan.

Application of IT

This section includes six important programmes–projects. Each programme will be shown in the form of a system of projects that will be carried out in two stages between 1996 and 2000. Below is a list of some important programmes in the application on IT.

1. Establishing a system of national databases and state management information. This is one of the tasks that should be given top priority in the 1996–2000 plan. This programme will be implemented through six large application projects of IT in important fields as the

Government Office, the Ministry of Planning and Investment, the General Statistical Department, the Ministry of Finance, and a system of state management informatization projects in all ministries, branches and fifty-three provinces and cities. This programme – project will be closely co-ordinated with the National Administrative Reform programme.

2. IT in the field of security and national defence. The application scope of IT in the fields of security and national defence is very large and has unique characteristics. Therefore, in order to modernize and strengthen National Defence and Security, the state should attach great importance to investment in two large projects in this field sponsored by the Ministry of Defence and the Ministry of Internal affairs, and earmark part of the national budget for National Defence and Security.

3. Setting up a commercial and market information network. The commercial and free-market information network project could be based on standardization, upgrading and development of the existing information network of the Ministry of Trade, co-ordinated with the databases at the Vietnam Chamber of Commerce and Industry, the Pricing Committee of the government, trading companies and enterprises. The project proposes to ask the state to grant or support part of the initial investment.

4. Application of IT in modernization of production and service branches. This application programme is very diversified, including projects focusing on the following aspects:

   - Part or total automization of the whole production process in the form of CAD, CAM, and so on.
   - Informatization and electrification of industrial products, production of 'intelligent' products.
   - Application of IT in the upgrading and modernization of service, production and non-production activities, in the fields of communications, transport, tourism, aviation, insurance, and so on.

5. Application of IT to health care, cultural and social branches. This programme includes IT projects in the following fields:

    ●   Application of IT in health care for the population.
    ●   Application of IT in the management of the population, the workforce, objects of social, policies and family planning.
    ●   Application of IT in the management and preservation of the national cultural heritage.

Measures and Policies on Development of IT until the Year 2000

1. Capital investment. The demand for capital investment to realize the national programme on IT in the 1996–2000 period is relatively high compared with the spending possibility of the state budget. Though Vietnam cannot yet catch up with developed countries in the region which make a very large investment in the development of IT, the government should promulgate appropriate policies to mobilize both domestic and foreign capital sources for the establishment and development of IT according to a set plan. However, in the first stage of implementing the plan, as for important programmes–projects, there should be proper investment from the state budget (though at a minimum level) so that initial physical prerequisites can be created for the development of IT in Vietnam, so that, from the twenty-first century, the gap between the development of IT in Vietnam and in other ASEAN countries can be considerably narrowed.
2. Capital construction. The requirements for capital construction in the IT industry are closely linked with each period and each development content of IT up to the year 2000. The demand for capital construction investment will become very high when developing the IT industry, especially in the development of a hardware industry with a system of warehouses, enterprises and data communications, and a processing industry

with data communications centres and networks. Also approaching is the need for capital construction in the information calculation centres of all ministries, branches and in localities; schools and faculties specializing in IT training; and in research and development offices in the field of IT.

At the time of writing, because of the complexity of separating the demand for capital construction investment in IT from the general demand for capital construction, the estimation of the former is included in the investment plan for capital construction in ministries, branches, and localities, and the estimated demand for capital construction investment in conducting the national programme on IT will be included in the spending plan for capital construction for all activities of the Programme Steering Committee.

3. The financial plan. The estimated costs for implementing the programme in each year will be as shown in Table 8.1.

Table 8.1

Year	Expenditure demand for implementing main contents of the IT development plan 1996–2000 (millions VN$)	Notes
1996	467 365	Minimum demand for starting the plan
1997	850 000	
1998	1 100 000	The first year of the second phase
1999	1 600 000	Starting the project on the IT industry
2000	2 200 000	Finalizing the master plan of the programme
Total (million VN$)	6 217 365	

4. Policies on encouraging the development of IT. In order to accelerate the implementation speed of the 1996–2000 plan for the National Programme on IT, in the master plan until the year 2000 there have been proposals to urgently research and issue some following pressing policies and measures:

● Policies on a standard and open system.
● Measures and policies on the construction of an informatized information system.
● Policies on technological transfer and international co-operation.
● Policies on protection of intellectual property and royalties.

CONCLUSIONS

To date there has not been much co-operation between Vietnam and Australia in the IT field. Apart from a joint venture installing some Viba stations, Australia has not yet made large investment in this field. At the present time, Vietnam is badly need of co-operation in training informatics experts and computer software techniques. The development plan for IT in Vietnam is now being realized. It is hoped that, in the future, IT in Vietnam will become an attractive field in the eyes of foreign investors, including those from Australia.

9 Land Management in Vietnam

Nguyen Tien Nhuan

P32 ᑫ15
673 ᑫ24

INTRODUCTION

In terms of the total surface area, Vietnam is a medium-sized country, ranking 59th among the 200 countries in the world, but in terms of the population, it is a big country, ranking 13th in the world. This has resulted in a very small area per capita, being equal to a sixth of the world average level (0.45 ha), the same as Great Britain, Germany and the Philippines, and ranking 135th among the 200 countries in the world and 9th among ten South East Asian countries. The total land area in 1994 was 33 168 000 ha, of which agricultural land area accounts for 22.2 per cent; forestry land area, 30 per cent; special purpose land area, 3.4 per cent; residential land area, 2.2 per cent; and unused land area, 42.2 per cent.

Vietnam is an agricultural country (with more than 80 per cent of its population doing farm work), a limited land area and a large population. During the economic development and mechanism transition in the orientation of industrialization and modernization in Vietnam, in order to make full use of the land resources in the most efficient way, the following targets have been given top priority:

- Food and foodstuff safety for the whole society, and most efficient land use.
- Improving living and working standards for all people.
- Ecological–environmental preservation in the entire country.

In recent years, land has not been used efficiently, causing low productivity. The land use structure has been

81

arbitrarily changed and has not brought about high efficiency.

With a view to attracting foreign investment, Vietnam promulgated the Investment Law in 1987, according to which, relationships concerning land are regulated in accordance with the land law enacted by the Vietnamese state. The ordinance on the rights and obligations of foreign organizations and individuals renting land in Vietnam makes it clear that 'Foreign organizations and individuals making investment in Vietnam are subject to the law on foreign investment in Vietnam'.

LAND USE AND MANAGEMENT IN 1991–5

Agricultural Land Use

Agricultural land area up to the year 1994 was 7 367 200 ha, accounting for 22.2 per cent of the total area, and increased by 6 per cent since the year 1980, when the agricultural land area was 6 913 400 ha.

Of the total agricultural land area, in 1994, the area for planting annual trees was 5 463 000 ha, accounting for 74 per cent, of which the area for planting rice accounted for 57.4 per cent; the area for planting perennial trees was 1 347 700 ha, accounting for 18.2 per cent; the meadow area was 221 000 ha, accounting for 2.99 per cent; and the water surface area for aqua-product cultivation was 334 700 ha, accounting for 4.5 per cent.

Because of the pressure caused by natural population increases, the average agricultural area per capita reduced continuously from 1084 sq.m. in 1985, to 1052 sq.m. in 1993, and 1030 sq.m. in 1994.

The shift in the economic structure in agriculture resulted in a reduction of the area for growing annual plants from 86.4 per cent in 1980 to 76.3 per cent in 1990, and 74.2 per cent in 1994, and a doubling of the area for growing perennial plants from 7.9 per cent in 1980 to 18.3 per cent in 1994.

The land use coefficient went up from 1.4 times in 1985 to 1.6 times in 1994, rice productivity increased from 2870 kg per ha in 1985 to 3650 kg per ha in 1994, bringing total food output from 18.2 million tonnes in 1985 to 26.2 million tonnes in 1994, of which rice output was 23.5 million tonnes in 1994.

From a position of having to import 500 000–800 000 tonnes of rice each year, Vietnam has now become the third largest rice exporter, selling over 2 million tonnes abroad in 1995, and having the possibility of exporting as many as 3 million tonnes of rice in 1998. However, the winter-harvest land has not been made full use of to plant short-term subsidiary crops (for example, tomatoes, cucumbers, garlic, potatoes, chillies, and so on) for export and domestic consumption.

Food processing equipment in particular, and the physical infrastructure for agriculture in general, while having been somewhat improved, are still backward. As a consequence, agriculturaral products for export and domestic consumption are mostly roughly processed, resulting in a low value and efficiency.

Forestry Land Use

By the year 1994, the whole country had 9 915 100 ha of forest, of which natural forests accounted for 8 810 000 ha and artificial forests the rest. Because of a loose forest management system that persisted for a long time, the area of forest and forest land in the northern mountainous and highland provinces of Vietnam decreased considerably in the 1980–90 period, causing adverse effects on the ecology and environment. The forest-covered area was very low in some provinces, such as Son La (10.7 per cent), Lai Chau (10.2 per cent), Lao Cai, Cao Bang, Lang Son, and so on. At the same time, total forest area was reduced by 247 000 ha on average annually while the afforestation area reached only an average number of 30 000 ha per year.

Since 1990, especially since the promulgation of the law on forest preservation and development, and thanks to the ongoing implementation of Project No. 327, the area of land and forest land has increased by 130 000 ha per year on average, and the forest land contracting system has brought about satisfactory results. Because of strict forest management to protect the environment, illegal and over-whelming timber exportation has been restricted to some extent in recent years. The export of processed timber has been encouraged while exported raw timber has been limited.

Special-purpose Land Use

Special purpose land is identified in land law as 'the land that is not used for agriculture, forestry, residence, includ-ing land for building industrial, scientific, technical works, transportation network, hydraulic system, dikes, social, cultural, educational, health care, gymnastic and sports and service projects; land to meet defence and security requirements; land for exploitation and exploitation of minerals, stone, sand; land to produce salt, ceramic wares, bricks, tiles and other construction materials; land where historic and cultural relics are located, beauty spots and landscapes, cemeteries, and land having water surface to be used in other purposes than agriculture'.

In Vietnam, the land area of this kind by the year 1994 accounted for only 3.39 per cent (that is 1 122 184 ha) of the total natural land area, of which land for construction made up 10.5 per cent; land for the transportation network, 19.8 per cent; and land for hydraulic systems, 32.8 per cent. In recent years, the area of special-purpose land has seen a considerable increase, averaging 37 498 ha per year in the 1990–4 period, of which land for trans-portation and hydraulic networks went up by about 6000 ha per year each.

Residential Land (Rural and Urban Areas)

Vietnam in 1996 had a population of 76 million, of which the number of people living in urban centres was

13 945 500, with the rest living in rural areas. The residential land in the entire country includes as a system of 500 urban centres, of which thirteen cities are under central control, seventy-three cities, towns and provinces, more than 400 townlets and districts, and tens of thousands of rural residential areas.

Most of the urban areas formed spontaneously around factories, enterprises or along national highways. According to 1994 estimates, the total residential area in the whole country was 717 507 ha, of which the urban areas accounted for 63 302 ha.

Present Difficulties

The development of industrial zones, especially in the fields of agriculture, forestry, aqua products and other key branches is in the initial stage, but sources of capital and raw material, as well as production and consumption areas, have not yet been firmly and sustainably formed on economic, scientific and technical bases.

Currently, agricultural and forestry exports account for about 30 per cent of the export value of the whole country, but as much as 70 per cent of these are roughly processed, resulting in a low export value and efficiency. In order to create processed exports there needs to be a large amount of capital and investment.

PLANNING ORIENTATIONS AND LAND USE PROSPECTS TO 2010

In order to reach the target of increasing by five times GDP per capita, the total agricultural land (7 367 200 ha in 1994) should reach 8 821 000 ha by the year 2010, showing an increase of 19 per cent. Forestry land, which was 9 915 100 ha in 1994 should increase to 16 245 800 ha, up by 63.1 per cent. Special purpose land, being 1 122 200 ha in 1994, should be 1 583 200 by the year 2010, growing by 4.1 per cent. Urban residential areas, being 146 070 ha in

1994, should reach 200 700 ha, increasing by 37.4 per cent. The rural residential area needs to increase from 654 200 ha to 799 500 ha by the year 2010, up by 6.2 per cent, and finally the unused area should be reduced by 39 per cent, from 13 982 200 ha in 1994 to 5 460 500 ha by the year 2010.

There should be good management of land use in agriculture and forestry, a rational and effective planting structure, and especially there should be plans for investment in farm and forestry product processing equipment, so that the objectives of increasing by five times the present export and domestic consumption value, ensuring food and foodstuff security, and preserving the ecological environment in the whole country can be reached.

PROSPECTS FOR FOREIGN INVESTORS

In the industrial field, Vietnam has made considerable steps forward thanks to its own efforts and to foreign investment, but it faces a lot of challenges that need to be solved as soon as possible in land management and production, and the processing of farm and forestry products for export and local consumption. With its strengths in terms of management and capital, Australia is in a favourable position to penetrate this field, and especially to invest in farm and forestry product processing activities in medium- and small-sized enterprises. Australia has already invested in a dairy farm and a milk factory in the South, a joint venture manufacturing furniture, and so on. Regarding urban development, Australia has entered into joint ventures with Vietnam to establish a design construction and development company in Ho Chi Minh City and a house construction company in Ha Noi which are operating well. In the future, Australia can also be involved in urban construction, infrastructural improvement in tourism resorts, and restoration of ancient streets, beauty spots, landscapes and historic relics.

10 Vietnam's Mineral, Oil and Gas Resources: Perspectives to the Year 2000

Nguyen Gia Kim

INTRODUCTION

Energy and Minerals

In Vietnam, there are various minerals such as coal, iron ore, bauxite, apatite, rare earth, and so on, but they are generally located in areas with undeveloped infrastructure and difficult exploitation conditions with, in addition, medium- and small-scale reserves. As assessed, Vietnam's metal reserve index is only 0.1, while Thailand's is 0.7, the Philippines' and Indonesia's each 1.54, and China's as high as 8.39. Vietnam has abundant hydro power resources in the north as well as in the south and a relatively large gas and oil potential. This is a considerable resource for the economic development of Vietnam. Some minerals are forecast to have relatively large reserves in Vietnam.

Vietnam has an abundant resource of limestone and clay for cement production, with several large deposits, mainly in the north. There are sand and gravel deposits, stone for construction and clay for making bricks relatively evenly distributed throughout the country, except in a few places in the Mekong River delta, with a potential of 1.5 billion tonnes.

There are fire-resistant materials such as refractory kaolin, alumina and quarzite, with considerable reserves. The kaolin clay for ceramic and porcelain manufacture has a potential of 200 million tonnes, and sand is also plentiful. In respect of minerals for building materials, Vietnam is ranked among the countries with the largest reserves in the world.

Vietnam's coal is concentrated mainly in the Quang Ninh coalfield, with an explorable reserve of about 2.2 billion tonnes. Most of it is anthracite, which is popular for industrial use in many countries. Vietnam is poor in fat coal, which is distributed in many small deposits, and the long-flame coal needed for cement production has a reserve of about 100 million tonnes only. In the Red River delta there is also a large resource of lignite, with a forecast reserve of 128 billion tonnes, lying at a depth of between 200 m and 2000 m in the rice planting zones.

Iron ore is centrally located, mainly in the Thach Khe deposits of Ha Tinh province and other provinces such as Thai Nguyen, Hoang Lien Son, Ha Giang and Cao Bang, with a total explorable reserve of 860 million tonnes and a content of 60–62 per cent (Thach Khe), most of which is magnetite. Being located next to the seashore, the exploitation conditions of Thach Khe deposit are difficult as it needs measures to prevent the penetration of sea water and a large volume of water from underground sources. The ore reserve is approximately 5–6 million tonnes per year.

Titanium, manganese, chromite and rare earth have moderate reserves. The following are forecast reserves: titanium, 20 million tonnes, most of them alluvial ore; manganese, 3 million tonnes in Cao Bang, where the ore contains a lot of silica and is of low quality; and chromite; 19 million tonnes have been explored, of which 2 million tonnes have a chromic oxide content of 47–51 per cent and contain a lot of finely granulated iron, causing difficulty in processing. The rare earth ore has a forecast reserve of 20 million tonnes and an explorable reserve of 10 million tonnes, most of which belong to the 'light' group, accompanied by barite, uranium and thorium. This is a very large potential, far surpassing the Vietnam's needs.

There are such non-ferrous metals as bauxite, tin, copper, lead and zinc. The forecast reserve of bauxite is 50 million tonnes, mainly in the north, in Ha Giang, Cao Bang and Lang Son provinces, with the largest deposits being located in the Central Highlands, with a forecast reserve of more than 10 billion tonnes and over 100 million tonnes for each deposit, distributed centrally in the zones of Dac Nong and Bao Loc, with aluminum oxide content of 38–43 per cent, even up to 45 per cent in some places. The deposits are strip mines under a thin ground layer, and therefore easy to exploit. Tin has a forecast reserve of 135 thousand tonnes, explorable of 86 thousand tonnes, being mainly alluvial ore, located in Tinh Tuc, Tam Dao and Qui Hop. Copper's forecast reserve is 4.35 million tonnes, concentrated mainly in the Sinh Quyen mine in Lao Cai province. The forecast reserve for lead and zinc is 4.35 million tonnes, mainly in Bac Thai province, with lead content of 1–6 per cent and zinc of 3–20 per cent.

Vietnam has a large source of apatite in the Cam Duong deposit (Lao Cai province), with a forecast reserve of over 2 billion tonnes, explored 390 million tonnes, out of which there are 41 million tonnes of grade 1 ore with P_2O_5 content of 32–41 per cent, which can be used directly to produce double super phosphate.

Oil and Gas

Vietnam has more than 3200 km of coastline and a large continental shelf, equal to three times the inland area, with a large potential of gas and oil reserves being exploited having a capacity of 8 million tonnes per year. There are large oil fields offshore in the south such as Bach Ho, Dai Hung and Rong, and so on.

Briefly speaking, then, the mineral and hydrocarbon potential of Vietnam is very large but it has not been exploited because of a shortage of capital, and exploitation and processing technology.

DEMAND FOR IMPORTED ENERGY AND FORECASTS

The need of Vietnam to import minerals at present and in the future to meet the requirements of production and construction is very large. Although Vietnam has exported crude oil, it still has to import 5–6 million tonnes of refined oil each year. Vietnam also has to import yearly tens of thousands of tonnes of fat coal and up to 500 000 tonnes of steel and iron for industrial use. In spite of having met a demand for building steel of 1 million tonnes per year, it has to import specialized steel to serve domestic production. Recently, tens of thousands of tonnes of raw material steel have been imported for production in steel mills.

Kaolin and gypsum are imported from Laos, in quantities of 50–70 thousand tonnes per year, and the yearly imported quantity of copper, lead and zinc is 5–7 thousand tonnes. While rich in apatite, Vietnam has to import yearly 200–300 thousand tonnes in the form of nitrogen and phosphorus (NP) and nitrogen, phosphorus and potassium (NPK), and so on. The need for imported non-ferrous metals such as copper, lead, zinc and aluminium will remain large up to the year 2010.

The prime concern now of the Vietnam government is to seek capital for the exploitation and processing of its minerals.

ENERGY SUPPLY (PRODUCTS FOR HOME USE AND EXPORT) AND FORECASTS

In previous years (1980–90), the main exported product of Vietnam was coal (anthracite) from the Quang Ninh mines, with a quantity of 788 thousand tonnes in 1990. The highest export quantity in recent years is over 2 million tonnes.

The present coal output is over 5 million tonnes per year, but because of the large requirement of domestic consumption, the maximum export quantity can only reach

2 million tonnes. Vietnam's coal importers are mainly Asian countries, such as Japan, Korea, China and so on.

The quantity of tin from the Tinh Tuc (Cao Bang) deposit is not great, but is favoured by many countries because of its high quality. The export quantity in 1990 was 1808 tonnes, and the highest quantity exported so far has reached over 5000 tonnes. The Lao Cai apatite mine has produced and exported over 10 000 tonnes of raw ore to Eastern European countries, and has also exported a small quantity of minerals such as chromite, coastal sand and rare earth each year.

The commodity having the biggest export quantity of Vietnam in recent years is crude oil, the export turnover of which reaches US$1 billion per year, being as much as a fifth of the export value of the whole country. The export quantity increases regularly year after year from 2 617 000 tonnes in 1990 to 7 562 000 tonnes in 1995, and up to about 8 200 000 tonnes in 1996.

What Vietnam has to face and overcome in exporting raw minerals are transport difficulties and low export value, leading to low economic effectiveness.

ENERGY PROSPECTS AND FORECASTS TO 2010

BHP's large project for oil and gas is currently under development (in the central offshore lots nos 120 and 121). BHP has co-operated with other companies to formulate a feasibility study of transportation and the treatment of the Nam Con Son field. Anzoil Corporation (Australia) has entered into a joint venture to carry out the exploration of the inland basin of Red River to exploit minerals.

The Ministry of Industry has issued permits to explore deposits for Australian companies (for example, Sinh Quyen copper mine, Lao Cai; Hinh River gold mine, Phu Yen; Cho Don lead–zinc mine, Bac Thai; Tra Nang gold mine, Lam Dong; and Luong Son gold mine, Hoa Binh). Some other Australian companies have also applied to search for gold in Lai Chau, Da Lat, Ninh Thuan, Binh

Thuan, Song Ma, Thanh Hoa, Nghia Lo and Quang Ninh, and are waiting for the Vietnamese government's approval for a mineral development strategy.

With regard to chemicals, BHP is preparing a project to establish an electricity nitrogen union to produce a million tonnes of urea fertilizer from the natural gas of Nam Con Son.

In the field of energy, there have been remarkable results and effectiveness in the classification and beneficiation of coal in Cua Ong–Cam Pha. A beneficiation factory is under construction in Nam Cau Trang–Hong Gai. A joint venture to produce and package emulsion explosives will be set up. The Australian flexible framework technology for supports in mining tunnels has been applied in Vietnam to raise the speed of tunnel excavation and to lower costs.

In order to develop the mineral exploitation and processing aiming at the implementation of industrialization and modernization of the country in the coming years, Vietnam needs a great deal of capital, more advanced equipment, and operating and management experience from Australia. Trade relations between Vietnam and Australia are stable, even though they have not been established for very long. At present, Vietnam exports crude oil, marine products, textiles and garments to Australia, and imports from Australia electrical devices, telecommunications and mining equipment, means of transport, chemicals and so on. The trade balance is temporarily in favour of Vietnam and will be improved when Australia increases its investment in the exploitation and processing of mineral resources of Vietnam, especially in oil and gas, and non-ferrous metals.

APPENDIX: THE OIL AND GAS INDUSTRY OF VIETNAM

Foreign Investment in Oil and Gas in Vietnam

Vietnam's law on foreign investment has attracted investment capital from several countries. From 1988 to the end of 1995, 1604 projects were granted investment licences with a total registered investment capital of US$18 834 million, divided as in the table below.

Oil and gas: by June 1996, Vietnam had signed twenty-nine product-sharing contracts (PSC) with Asian, Australian, European and North American companies, almost all of which are contracts to seek offshore oil and gas, with a total capital of about US$1.3 billion. In April 1994, a consortium of companies headed by Mobil signed an agreement for the rights to search and produce in the Thanh Long field, Lot No. 5.1b. This noted the return of US oil companies after a nineteen-year economic embargo.

Results of Oil Exploitation

Table 10.2 shows that there are three oil fields under operation at present, namely Bach Ho, Dai Hung and Rong. In ten years the Bach Ho field has produced more than 80 per cent of Vietnam's total exported crude oil output. Its exploitation capacity is approaching the maximum of 150 000 bpd. This is one of the largest fields in the South East Asia region. None the less, it needs modern technologies to ensure the exploitation stability of the Bach Ho field and to increase its output to optimum exploitation effectiveness.

Table 10.1

	1988	*1989*	*1990*	*1991*	*1992*	*1993*	*1994*	*1995*
Number of investment projects	37	70	111	155	193	272	362	404
Amount of investment capital (US$ millions)	366	539	596	1388	2271	2987	4071	6616

Table 10.2   Product-sharing contracts carried out up to January 1996

No.	Investment company	Lot no. and basin zone	Field	Note
1	AEDC (Japan)	5.3 Con Son	Moc Tinh	Gas found
2	ANZOIL (Australia)	Tien Hai	Tien Hai	Gas field
3	British Gas (UK)	4.1 Con Son	Dong Nai River	Geologic study
4	BP (UK)	5.2 Con Son 6.1 Con Son	Hai Than Kim Cuong Tay	Gas found Oil and gas found
5	BHP (Australia)	51A Con Son	Dai Hung	Oil and gas field
6	Canada	12W Con Son		Oil not found
7	Enterprise	17 Offshore Con Son	Cam	Oil found
8	Idennitsui (Japan)	102 per 91 Hanoi Concave		Abandoned Sept. 1995
9	IPC (Canada)	115 Xingchai		Will be abandoned
10	Japan-Vietnam Petro	15.2 Cuu Long	Rang dong	Oil found
11	Lasmo (UK)	4.2 Con Son	Soi bien	Under assessment
12	Mobil	5.1B Con Son	Thanh Long	Oil and gas found
13	Occidental (USA)	4.3 Con Son		
14	OMV (Austria)	104 Hanoi		
15	Pedco (Korea)	11.2 Con Son	Rong doi	Oil and gas found
16	P. Fina (Belgium)	465051 Ma Lai		
17	Petronas (Malaysia)	1.2 Cuu Long	Rubyprospect	Oil & Gas are found

Table 10.2   continued

No	Investment company	Lot no. and basin zone	Field	Note
			Emerald 1	Oil and gas found
18	Shell (Holland)	10. Offshore Con Son		Under assessment
19	Total (France)	11.1 Offshore Con Son	Cache	Oil and gas found
20	Viersovpetro	9.16 Cuu Long	Bach Ho Rong	Oil and gas field

After two years of exploitation, the Dai Hung field showed a reserve of 100 million barrels, far below the estimated reserve of 700 million barrels. Therefore the field output has reduced by 50 per cent to 17 000–18 000 bpd (previously 35 000 bpd).

Being exploited from late 1994, the Rong field has characteristics similar to those at the Bach Ho field, with an estimated oil reserve of 100–150 million bdp. At the time of writing, the capacity is under 10 000 bpd, or equal to 8 per cent of the daily oil output of Vietnam.

Results of Gas Exploitation

Vietnam has begun its 'Project of Bach Ho gas use' plan, part of Vietnam's master plan for gas production and usage. According to the plan, natural gas will be used as fuel for electricity plants, producing fertilizers and for other industries.

The project consists of:

1. A gas gathering system in the Bach Ho field.
2. Main pipeline from the central treatment system to the inland.
3. A gas treatment factory in Dinh Co.

4. Storage of liquid and service facilities for export on Thi Vai river.
5. Inland pipeline to Thu Duc, suburb of Ho Chi Minh City.

The construction of a 16-inch diameter pipeline from the Bach Ho oil field to Ba Ria–Vung Tau was completed, to supply 1 million cbm of natural gas per day for the first gas fuelled electricity plant in Ba Ria. Phase II of the project will be to transport gas from Ba Ria to Thu Duc via the inland pipeline, and the construction of an LPG factory and an offshore gas compressing station which was put into operation on May 1997. The entire project was completed in 1997. Some characteristic of Vietnam's crude oil are given in Table 10.3.

Vietnam's Oil and Gas Outlook

The Vietnam continental shelf has a large oil and gas potential which has not yet been explored. Some of the zones of the shelf are the Bac Bo gulf, the central zone, and the south and south-west of the country. More than 650 000 sq.km of the area is considered to have gas and oil potential offshore and this has been divided into 170 lots. Only 25 per cent of them have been explored to date, with about 180 wells being drilled since the early 1980s. Vietnam is opening offshore Lot Nos. 15.1, 120, 130, and the areas

Table 10.3   Characteristics of Vietnam crude oil in the fields being exploited

	Bach Ho	Dai Hung	Rong
API gravity index	40.9	34.2	22.1
Sulphur content	0.03	0.08	0.1
Nickel and vanadium (millionth)	1.1	4.0	12.1
Nitrogen (millionth)	300	400	300
Flowing point	36.0	33.5	26

in Lot Nos. 9 and 16. The adjacent Lot Nos. 122–130 running from the coastal area next to Quy Nhon towards the south as far as area No. 300 in the east of the Con Son concave area have been investigated geophysically, of which Lot Nos. 9, 15.1 and 16 have been explored and considered as an area with a good gas and oil outlook.

In 1997, the commercial production of the Mitsubishi Rang Dong field began in the Cuu Long sedimentary basin, near the Bach Ho oil field. The Rang Dong crude oil field has an API gravity index of 38 and a sulphur content of 0.05 per cent and is being drilled to evaluate reserve capacity.

In 1998, the Thanh Long field will come into operation, with an estimated output of 50 000 bpd. This field was found by a Japanese consortium and considered to have a lot of gas and may contain up to 600 million barrels of oil.

Almost all places where oil is found are located in the Con Son and Cuu Long basins, so it is almost certain that there will be plenty of oil and gas found in Lot Nos. 9, 15.1 and 16. The new fields being developed, such as Rang Dong and Thanh Long, will compensate for the drop in output of the Bach Ho field.

New Discoveries of Gas

British Petroleum (BP) found three large gas fields in the Con Son basin within two years (1994 and 1995), and there will certainly be more gas discoveries in the future. The Bach Ho gas field has not been fully exploited. In the Con Son basin, gas has been found by Japanese Arabian Oil in Lot No. 5.3, by Lasmo in Lot No. 4.2, by Total in Lot No. 11.1, and by Korean Pedco in Lot No. 11.2. These discoveries will be examined for commercial use once evaluation results prove the field potential.

The most important event in the Con Son area is the discovery of gas in BP's Lot No. 6.1 at Lan Do and Lan Tay. That is not pure, liquidized petroleum gas (LPG) but its quality is high and its potential is estimated at about 2000 billion cu.ft. The production of natural gas will start in the year 1998, with an output of about 200 million cu.ft per day at maximum. BP is now preparing for a US$600 million project of to develop building facilities at sea, a recovery system and a pipeline to transport gas from inland areas to Vung Tau for commercial use.

BP is also searching for gas in Lot No. 5.2 under a co-ordinated programme with Statoil. In the middle of 1995, these companies declared the discovery of a great quantity of gas in the Con Son area. The Hai Than well has gas at a depth of 2900 m in Lot No. 5.2. Checks of drilling hole have proved that gas is of high quality.

In late 1996, an LPG plant with a capacity of 300 000 tonnes was put into operation. In the period 1996–2000, Vietnam will develop some liquidized natural gas (LNG) plants; one or two plants to produce urea fertilizers with a capacity of 500 000 tonnes per year; and build an electricity plant using gas worth US$810 million situated in the Ba Ria–Vung Tau province. By the end of the 1996–2000 plan, Vietnam will have a possibility of exporting a large quantity of LPG.

In late 1996, Vietnam set up a 6.5 million tonne oil refinery with an investment capital of about US$1.2 billion in Dung Quat (Central Vietnam).

Forecast on the Oil Exploitation Capacity of Vietnam to the Year 2010

In the specialists' opinion, the Thanh Long and Rang Dong fields will be exploited in the late twentieth century, and the crude oil capacity of Vietnam will reach 400 000 bpd in the year 2000 and 700 000 bpd in 2005.

Estimated Investment Capital for Oil and Gas Development of Vietnam in the Period 1996–2000

According to the records of the Ministry of Planning and Investment, by the end of 1995 the registered capital amount of licensed projects was about US$19.35 billion, and the operational capital about US$5.5 billion (28 per cent). An

Table 10.4   Forecast of crude oil in Vietnam oil fields, in 1000 bpd

Year	Bach Ho	Rong	Dai Hung	Thanh Long	Rang Dong
1995	140	15	35	n.a.	n.a.
2000	150	25	100	50	100
2005	110	20	175	200	250
2010	60	10	120	200	200

Source: Global Pacific and Partners, 1995.

amount of US$9–10 billion out of the US$14 billion remainder can be realized in the period 1996–2000. About US$4–5 billion will not materialize because of lack of feasibility, expiration, or the release for the licence of the projects. Out of US$19.35 billion, there is US$1.215 billion for explorable drilling of oil and gas exploitation and gas pipelines, comprising twenty-four projects.

In the period 1996–2000, an estimated minimum investment capital of about US$15–17 billion can be realized (including investment capital transferred from the period 1991–5) which is distributed for oil and gas development as follows:

- To develop commercial oil and gas fields, including pipelines for oil and gas, and refinery plant No. 1 — US$2.5–3 billion
- LPG plant — US$0.4 billion
- Electricity plants — US$0.5–1 billion
- Urea fertilizer plant — US$0.5–0.6 billion.

In the specialists' opinion, capital for oil and gas development in the period 2001–2010 will be about US$10–12 billion, comprising the following:

- Explorable and exploiting drilling.
- Installation of oil and gas pipelines to the coast to facilitate the export of oil and gas.

● LPG plant.
● Electric plant using gas.
● Urea fertilizer chemical plant.

Oil and gas exploitation in Vietnam is of great importance to its economic development from now until the year 2010. The development of Vietnam's oil and gas industry requires high technology and advanced equipment, and needs the assistance of countries having oil and gas technologies, such as the USA, Japan, Germany, France and so on, and joint ventures and co-operation with foreign countries in financing the projects.

11 Vietnam's Post and Telecommunications Prospects

Nguyen Duong

C86

P31

GENERAL BACKGROUND

Prior to 1990, the technology of Vietnam's Post and Telecomunications (P&T) network was very backward. The switching systems throughout the country were all rudimentary electromechanical automatic exchanges, single station. The automatic exchanges, which were considered to be the most modern in Vietnam at that time, were the electromechanical ones of AT2-64 and AT3-65 types made in the former German Democratic Republic (GDR). By the end of 1990 there were only about 10 000 telephones in the network, a ratio of 0.18 telephones per 100 people, one of the lowest rates in the world.

From 1991–5, the P&T services grew rapidly. The number of telephones in 1991 was 140 000, rising to 183 000 for 1992, and up to 778 000 by the year 1995. The average ratio in the year 1992 was 0.23 telephones per 100 people, and in 1995 it was 1.05. At the time of writing, nearly 60 per cent of communities have no telephone. With present demand, from the year 1996, about 500 000 telephones must be installed additionally each year, producing a ratio of 3–5 telephones per 100 people by the year 2000.

Regarding mobile communications, a digital GMS of European standard with 30 000 phones has been installed and is operational in twenty districts throughout the country. The mobile communications market is estimated to reach a value of US$250 million in 1998.

The technological basis of the P&T is being modernized increasingly. The earth satellite stations of A standard transmitting north–south axis information by fibre optic cables with a capacity of 34 MPS, a wide band digital microwave system for Hanoi–Ho Chi Minh City of 140 MPS, and digital switching exchanges Alcatel 1000 E 10. EWSO, AXE 03 TDX-113 have been installed in Hanoi and Ho Chi Minh City.

To meet the telecommunications equipment demand, four factories with modern technologies were built between 1991–5 to produce copper cables with oil, digital microwave and exchange fibre optic cables, and digital telephones.

VIETNAM'S P&T MARKET

Despite the fast growth rate of Vietnam's P&T, because of a very low beginning point, a big investment is needed in the future to catch up with the advanced level of the rest of the world. According to foreign investors' evaluation, Vietnam's P&T market is the most promising one in Asia. The investment into Vietnam's postal infrastructure is very attractive because of its large needs, high growth rates and fast payback period. Vietnam's telecommunications can be modernized immediately because it is possible to apply the world's advanced technologies. According to the Vietnam Post Company's estimated costs, the value of Vietnam's telecommunications equipment market will increase to US$420 million (this was US$158 million in 1993). Vietnam's quantity of international calls has increased at an extraordinary rate every year: there were 2300 international channels in 1996 from only nine in 1995, and the volume of international calls increased from 3 million minutes per year to 200 million minutes per year in 1996.

Between the years 1996–2000, Vietnam's P&T will make new strides in the fields of computers and telecommunications, attaching great importance to digitalization to prepare for multimedia service development. It is envisaged to set up a 565 MPS Thailand–Vietnam–Hong Kong international marine cable line with a capacity of 7000 channels; to build a China–Laos–Vietnam–Malaysia–Singapore inland fibre optic cable line; to build a Vietnam–Philippines international marine optic cable line; and to continue the extension of satellite stations both in the INTERSPUTNIK and INTERSAT systems. In domestic telecommunications, the intended works are building a fibre optic cable line on the 500 KV electric line with SDH-2.5 Gb/s with 30 000 phone channels; upgrading the fibre optic cable system along National Route No. 1A from Hanoi to Ho Chi Minh City from PDH-34 Mb/s to SDH-2.5 Gb/s technology; building a domestic marine fibre optic cable line of SDH-622 Mb/S-SDH-2.5 Gb/s; quickly developing new telecommunications services, such as expanding mobile communications services for the whole country; integrating into the regional and world's network; and rapidly increasing videophone services, television conferences, faxes, data transmissions, and cables for possibly up to 85 million people by the year 2000. Vietnam is an attractive telecommunications market for foreign investors.

PROSPECTS FOR AUSTRALIA TO THE YEAR 2000

Vietnam's P&T has had a close relationship with Australia for a long time. In 1987, Telstra (formerly OTCI) signed the first agreement with Vietnam Post-Office (VNPT). Since then Australia has always been an important investment partner of Vietnam's in the field of P&T. Vietnam is co-operating with Australia in building a Thailand–Vietnam–Hong Kong optic cable marine line. Another joint venture between Vietnam and Australia exploits paging services in Ho Chi Minh City. A project to set up laws on P&T covering the two parties has finished Phase I and will continue to Phase II.

Among the commodities imported from Australia, telecommunications machinery and equipment are very important. Apart from the production of some simple conductive wires, Vietnam has to import all telecommunications equipment, mainly from France, Korea, Australia, and recently from the USA. Vietnam is also learning to produce transmitting equipment, digital microwaves, fibre optic cables, switching equipment, digital electronics, accessing rotary switching exchange cables for internal use, plastic pipes for cables, and terminal conductive equipment for optic cables. Vietnam needs the co-operation of Australia very much in this area.

Vietnam's P&T market is also attractive for foreign investors, including Australians. This results from many years of relations of these investors' countries with Vietnam's P&T. These investors can be involved in large projects of the radio and television companies, banks, insurance, state treasures, custom offices, and tax organizations.

Vietnam's P&T is a very young industry with regards to technology. In addition to the shortage of investment capital (the financial fund of the P&T Corporation is about US$250 million), Vietnam very much needs a body of qualified workers and experts. Australia has contributed significantly to the field of training. The creation of a body of qualified workers is useful, first for Vietnam as it lacks specialists, and useful in the long term for the introduction of Australian goods, and the facilitation of Australian investment in Vietnam.

Investment and trade promotion is very necessary for understanding the market between the two countries. Australia is a leading country with several achievements in the field of P&T. This is an advantage. However, in order to meet Vietnam's telecommunications demands, Australian investors need to commit to long-term and continous strategy. Some big companies such as Motorola (USA), Korea Telecom (Korea). Ericsson (Sweden), Nokia (Japan) and Siemens (Germany) are competing in the field of Vietnam's P&T at the present time.

Vietnam is on the way to industrialization and integration, step by step, in regional and global communities. To develop P&T is one of the important preconditions to implementing its targets. To expand co-operation with Australia in this field will certainly be of great advantage to both countries. Actual and forecast requirements of Vietnam's P&T are given in Table 10.5.

P&T development objectives to the year 2000

Table 11.1   P&T developing objectives to the year 2000

No	Parameters	1992	1995	2000	Notes
1	Telephone density (no. of phones/ 100 people)	0.26	Alternative 1:0.76 Alternative 2:1.00	2.5 3.0	1995: 74 million people
2	Total number of telephones on the line (no. of phones)	170.00	Alternative 1:560 000 Alternative 2:740 000	2 000 000 2 400 000	2000: 80 million people
3	Local antomatization	3/53 T 0%	100%	100%	
4	Digitalization of network (IDN)	2%	90%	100%	
5	Long-distance automatization (STD, IDD)	39.3%	90%	100%	
6	Multi-service digitalization (ISDN)	0%	0%	5%	
7	Number of post-offices	1779	Alternative 1:2000 Alternative 2:2300	3000 3500	
8	Radio coverage By territory By population	0% 0%	92% 97%	100% 100%	
9	Television coverage By territory By population	0% 0%	60% 72%	100% 100%	

12 Privatization of Vietnamese Enterprises

L33
P31

Pham The Tho

BACKGROUND

The ten year-period (1986–96) of Vietnam's economic renovation has been a process of shifting from a bureaucratic command economy into a market one with many sectors. They are state-owned enterprises, joint ventures, domestic and foreign-invested joint ventures, limited companies, and trading households. The socialism-orientated economy has been following a market mechanism under state control.

The development of Vietnam's market economy has consolidated the market dominant role for some state enterprises. This has provided economic stability and crucial commodities to people such as rice, petroleum, steel, cement, sugar, paper, cooking salt, chemical fertilizers, and so on. At the same time, private enterprises, co-operatives, local and foreign-invested joint ventures, and foreign-funded companies free developed under the Corporate Law, the Foreign Investment Law, the Domestic Investment Law, and so on.

Maintaining the restructuring of the economic sectors according to the privatization trend, most state enterprises were not necessarily owned directly by the state, like industrial manufacturers (for example, electronics, electrics, garments, fabrics, vehicles and equipment), and particularly in developing individual retailers and service suppliers in local markets.

The Vietnam market in recent years, and especially in the 1990–5 period, has made significant steps forward:

1. We have reformed the markets for consumer goods, materials, services (also covering trading and legal consultancies), science and technology, economic information, labour, and so on. The capital and monetary markets have also been reformed.
2. Diversifying and stimulating the expansion of the different economic sectors is a most important issue in the creation and establishment of the new economy.

Thus the government of Vietnam has been building up a favourable economic environment for all sectors of the economy to participate in the commodity and service markets in various ways under existing laws. The privatization trend has resulted in the formation of small and medium-sized enterprises, taking form of limited companies, stock companies, private companies, trading households and co-operatives.

The development of private enterprises in Vietnam has proved to be on the right track, and necessary, because:

● Agricultural, forestry and aquatic products are strong elements of Vietnam's economy and have not yet been well exploited.
● About 80 per cent of the population lives in rural, forestry and fishing areas, with abundant human resources and cheap labour costs.
● Urban labour is also in surplus. The sources of goods and services have been underdeveloped.
● The Vietnamese attitude towards production investment has now changed. Having not restored gold and US dollar standards, as in the past, they are willing to invest capital into businesses or other profitable activities. There are about 2 million Vietnamese living abroad, providing a major money source that has helped relatives at home to invest money in profitable operations.

The development of private enterprises in the form of small and medium-sized enterprises is a necessity in the Vietnamese economy. Certainly, the criterion of a small or medium-scale enterprise comes from the conditions and circumstances of Vietnamese society.

CONDITIONS AND FORECASTS

Corporate Law, Private Business Law and Co-operative Law have been promulgated by the government of Vietnam, and trade law and other laws will be issued in due course to create an integrated mechanism for market economy developments.

Retail sales growth by the private sector in the economy is shown in Table 12.1.

As of December 1993, the total number of private enterprises had grown significantly from 1990 (see Table 12.2).

According to a survey of 1 July 1995; the total number of units were as shown in Table 12.3.

Table 12.1   Retail sales growth by the private sector

Year	Growth (VN$ billions)
1985	27.2
1986	138
1987	627
1988	3.646
1989	7.851
1990	12.723
1991	23.740
1992	38.800
1993	49.946
1994	69.952
1995	89.571

Table 12.2   Private enterprises in Vietnam, December 1993

	Number	Capital (in VN$)
Private enterprises	8 418	1 300
Limited liabilities Companies	3 217	2 188
Joint stock firms	103	568
Total	11 738	3 956

	Hanoi	Haiphong	Ho Chi Minh City
Private enterprises	340	102	595
Limited companies	631	155	1 411
Joint stock companies	9	4	48

	Northern	Central provinces	Southern	Mountainous
Private enterprises	2 198	2 149	7 391	491
Capital volume (VN$ billions)	811.5	466.2	2701.0	167.6

Table 12.3   Analysis of units

	Total	Capital construction industry	Hotel trading services	Other sectors
Private enterprises, Limited liability, Joint stock companies (Vietnamese)	14 971	6 311	8 011	649
Foreign-funded private firms	40	27	8	5

In general, over the 18-month run (12/1993–1/7/1995), the number of private businesses, limited liability companies, and joint-stock companies had increased as follows:

December 1993	11 738	
July 1995	14 971	(up 28 per cent).

The increase reflected a healthy and favourable economic environment for small and medium-sized private enterprises, on the following basis.

The View of the Vietnamese Government and Party on Medium and Small-Scale Enterprises

As in other countries in the world, the view of the Vietnam government and the party on medium and small-scale enterprises (SMEs) has strongly affected the development of these sectors. In the whole process of economic development, the growth of SMEs is always a concern of the government and the party of Vietnam.

Before 1986

Before 1986, with the aim of building a centrally-planned economy, SMEs worked as a supplement to state enterprises. This was particularly clear in the industrial field, which was divided into state industry and handicrafts.

Handicrafts are, more precisely, handicrafts and small industries. Most of the enterprises (mainly collectives and groups of collectives) in the sector still remain small-scale, both in terms of capital and the workforce. Hiring labour was strictly constrained because it was considered to be an action of exploitation.

The policy in general was unfair, between state industry and the handicraft and small-scale industrial sectors: handicrafts and small-scale enterprises were not supported by investment. Loans from the banks for these enterprises were restricted and at higher interest rates than the rates applied to the state industry. Even wages, bonuses and norms applied to workers in the enterprises of the sector were lower than those in state enterprises of the same type.

Development orientation in handicraft and small-scale enterprises was modelled after socialistic large-scale production, and their existence was considered temporary. Individual establishments were to move to collective ones, collectives of a low grade were to develop to collectives of higher grades, and collectives of a high grade, with necessary conditions, were to be converted into state enterprises. This perception have strongly affected the development of handicraft and small-scale enterprises. Facilities for collectives and groups of collectives were in a poor state after decades of construction. The managers were not trained, the workers were low-skilled, and a number of traditional professions had disappeared. As a result, most of the enterprises could not survive as the economy shifted to a market mechanism.

After 1986

The 6th National Convention of the Communist Party of Vietnam in 1986 advanced a policy of universal renovation, with an emphasis on economic renovation. The view has strongly affected the development of handicraft and small-scale enterprises. It is a recognition of the long-lasting existence of the various economic sectors in Vietnam. However, the policy over the non-state sectors has changed qualitatively since the Political Bureau of the Party promulgated Decision No. 16/NQ/TWO on 15 July 1988. The decision states:

(i)   The collective economy consists of various forms of low and high organization under the two basic degrees, with collectives and groups of collectives being socialistic economic components.

(ii) The household economy is additional work as processing contracts for firms and services done by government employees, state workers, collective and private firms, and people of non-working age.

(iii) State–private joint enterprises are economic establishments with capital contributed by one or several households and the government as wealth or money, or as stocks. Profits of firms are divided on the basis of capital contributed.

(iv) The private economy consists of firms whose promoters are people owning capital, and which operate under the law over the private economy:

- Individual households are productive units on the basis of family, possibly employing labour temporarily; and
- Small entrepreneurs are productive households with the breadwinners of the households being the main workers, and employing labour.

(v) An industrial capitalistic enterprise (private enterprise in short) is an enterprise with capital contributed by one or several national capitalists. The firms of this type operate as private businesses, private companies or joint stock companies with an unlimited size. They are eligible to hire labour on the basis of production and technique.

The government secures national capitalists doing business legally; actively contributing to the national plan, the people's life and the country's benefits by law. They are the members of Vietnam's Fatherland Front.

The above stated views affected the perception and policy of the Vietnamese government over SMEs. The fact that private enterprises are allowed to develop to an unlimited size and to employ labour on the basis of production and business has brought new opportunities for development. The term 'non-state industry' has become popular to replace the term 'handicraft and small-scale industry' that had been used commonly in the past.

In the non-state industry sectors, there have appeared a number of large enterprises such as the Minh Phung, Bitis and Huy Hoang companies in Ho Chi Minh City, employing thousands of workers and billions of Vietnam dollars for their business. Meanwhile, tens of thousands of state enterprises employ just tens of workers and limited amounts of capital. Clearly, with respect to scale, both the state and non-state sectors have medium- and small-scale firms. This shows that the policy is relevant to each form of enterprise and is urgently needed.

In the open economy, information comes in and out of Vietnam more freely. The status and successful development of SMEs in other countries have affected the view of the Vietnamese government over the sector in Vietnam. The enterprises in Vietnam are no longer considered as a supplement but rather an effective tool to solve socioeconomic problems, which contribute to the development of the country.

The Vietnamese Government's Existing Policy on SME Development

As has been mentioned above, the new concept of SME has not yet been defined clearly. However, the new views on these sectors have affected their development negatively. This is clear through the following points:

Research on SMEs has Attracted Concern by the Government and International Support

Immediately after the execution of the Political Bureau's Decision No. 16/NQ/TW in 1990, the Central Institute for Economic Management ran a number of workshops sponsored by Germany on medium- and small-scale firms, and then conducted surveys of over 135 enterprises of this type in the Ha Bac province. The province is organizing consultancy work for the development of the firms and setting up a system of credit guarantee to support the enterprises financially. ZDH-Tecnonet Asia also carried out a project financed by Germany on the development of SMEs in Vietnam. The country has also received a number of projects relating to the development of SMEs from the United Nations, including Project VIE/86 045, for training. As a result, thousands of small entrepreneurs are now equipped with the necessary knowledge to expand their businesses.

Apart from Germany and the United Nations, other countries have expressed their willingness to assist Vietnam to develop business. In September 1992, a delegation of medium- and small-scale industry executives from Taiwan visited Vietnam to study the market and explore opportunities for co-operation. The delegation signed a letter of understanding with its Vietnamese counterpart. During its visit to Vietnam in 1993, a delegation of the British Executive Service Overseas offered a list of 3000 specialists who were ready to help Vietnam in consultancy over the development of SMEs. Japan also sent a number of delegations, including senior managers from its medium- and small-scale industries to Vietnam to study co-operative possibilities.

Recognizing the important role played by SMEs, the government of Vietnam allowed a number of organizations to carry out surveys among them. The surveys have pointed out the characteristics, working environment, advantages and disadvantages of the enterprises in Vietnam. The most noticeable among the surveys was the one conducted by the Ministry of Labour and the Central Institute for Economic Management.

Legal Framework for Medium- and Small-scale Firms Has Been Established

A number of legal documents about SMEs were enacted after Decision No. 16/NQ/TW. The documents relate to non-state enterprises as well as to SMEs. Unlike the time before 1986, when SMEs were allowed to operate under collectives and groups of collective forms, they now have a large range of choices for their existence form. They can be private enterprises, companies, collectives, groups of collectives or business groups operating under Ordinance No. 66/HDBT.

Laws state clearly the obligations and the authority of the enterprises as well as the protection of their legal interests. In addition, regulations regarding tax and credits have been creating a lot of opportunities in their first stage of development. The existing policy of the Vietnamese government over non-state enterprises (mainly SMEs) is orientated towards controlling rather than supporting or promoting them. The enterprises are facing a number of problems in the way they conduct business.

The execution of related policies takes place slowly; some came into effect even years after first being advanced. This situation is even worse in remote provinces. All these reflect the limitations of civil servants. As a result, negative phenomena in the management of the firms still exist, particularly in activities relating to the procedures of granting business licences, rating taxes, guaranteeing credit and so on. Illegal intermediaries have appeared.

Bodies Supporting SMEs Have Been Established and Are Initially Developing Their Role

In recent years, as the government perceived the role played by the enterprises and their requirements, it allowed the setting up of a number of organizations to support SMEs. At the central level, three promoting centres are notable: namely, the centre under the Chamber of Commerce and Industry; the centre of the Council of Collective Unions; and the centre of the General Department for Standards and Quality. Although the centres still feel inexperienced in their work, they appear to offer a sensible help to SMEs.

The supporting centre under the Chamber of Commerce and Industry is primarily to solve questions affecting the criteria of classification, to expand international co-operation, and to seek financial sources and markets.

The centre under the Council of Collective Unions administers some training courses for the enterprises and issues some publications to disseminate information and to answer questions of concern. Although still in its organizational phase, the centre under the General Department for Standards and Quality offers services with an emphasis on helping the firms to deal with new technologies and techniques.

What is important at the moment is the co-ordination of the activities of the enterprises, directing them towards certain work and avoiding unnecessary overlap in their operations.

PROSPECTS BY 2010

Trade ties between Vietnam, Australia and other countries in the region have been strengthened further with growing two-way imports and exports. Since 1993, foreign trade between Vietnam and Australia has grown, and in 1993 alone soared nine-fold when compared with trade in 1990 (see Table 12.4).

Trade Promotion Campaign

Australia is an advanced industrial country that is geographically close to Vietnam. Vietnam's and Australia's governments have a planned trade enhancement policy. Vietnam's private enterprises will be able to produce and process commodities such as coffee, cashewnuts, mushrooms, livestock feed and fine art products. In return, Australian goods flowing into Vietnam's markets include flour, small information equipment, mechanical machinery, and small production lines that are suitable for the expansion of Vietnamese small and medium-sized businesses.

Training Experts in Trade and Business

According to a survey on 1 November 1994, the number of non-state enterprise managers totaled 10 735. Of these, undergraduates accounted for 5198; primary school graduates 271; secondary school graduates 1915; with the

Table 12.4   Trade between Vietnam and Australia, 1993–5, $A millions

	Exports to Australia	*Imports from Australia*
1993	115	251
1994	289.4	163.5
1995	329.1	197.9

remaining 3351 people being graduates from colleges and universities.

A major proportion of secondary school and university graduates are technical staff who went to work for private firms after retiring or leaving state-run enterprises, and their knowledge of trade and business is limited. Individual companies often run their commercial affairs with high risks. In the coming years, training courses on two or three days a week, with two hours per each period, on trade and business management should be held for private business-men. Each course should to last up to six months, with certificates awarded on the completion of the course. (Vietnamese trainees prefer certificates issued by an international organization.)

International Competition in Commerce

Vietnamese individual business has recorded successful achievements in the market. Prior to 1975, the former Saigon business market was rated higher than that in Thailand and South Korea, and was not inferior to Hong Kong.

Today and in the future, Vietanmese business can compete with the international market in farm products, food, consumer goods, handmade fine art items, cosmetics, and so on, provided that:

(a) Capital investment and investment policy should be supplemented to ensure long-term interest. (The Domestic Investment Law has not yet been devel-oped effectively.)

(b) High-tech production processing instruments can be purchased.

As Vietnamese businesses' advantages are cheap labour costs, and low-cost raw materials; and Vietnamese people are intelligent and sensible to the market if they are supplied with economic information regularly and promptly.

Marketing and Product Diversification Policy

Vietnam's private businesses are not yet in a position to access foreign markets. They seem to be inactive in the expansion of products in recent years (because of the reproduction of imported goods with some technical modifications). This is why Vietnamese business people should set up direct exchange links with Australian, ASEAN and other markets. Some enterprises have, however, processed food, particularly in the midlands, the mountainous and coastal regions.

Price Policy and Transportation Costs

Primary products transportation costs still account for a major proportion of manufacturing prices in Vietnam's market, because of poor traffic systems. This is an obstacle faced by business. But the price of goods and services in Vietnam is seen as being cheap compared with international market prices. The Vietnamese state does not regulate the prices fixed by private businesses. They are determined by the private businesses and the market. However, the government has been introducing policies affecting prices, such as tax reduction or exemption, preferential credit, and the government's price stabilization fund will facilitate enterprises' expansion and increase the production of goods and services.

Moving Towards Trade Strategies in Vietnam

Vietnam's economic strategies are aimed at the industrialization and modernization of the economy with the participation by the various economic sectors (state-run, non-state-run, and foreign business) under socialism-orientated state control. The development of production and services will obviously result in a market expansion inside and outside the country. On the international market, it is most likely to develop relations with the Asia-Pacific and Australian markets. Like other countries, Vietnam has carried out an open-door policy, integrating its economy with the world market in a bid to move towards trade liberalization.

The Law on Private Business, Corporate Law, Foreign Investment Law, Law on Domestic Investment Incentives and Trade Law were approved by early in 1998 will create a legal corridor for Vietnam's trade development.

GENERAL REMARKS

Vietnam's economic potential, excluding gas, oil, coal, farming, forestry and aquatic products, is still very plentiful and various.

Vietnam's economy has made firm steps towards a market economy. Non-state businesses have expanded strongly. The number of private businesses, limited liability, and joint-stock companies have grown by more than 20 per cent annually. At the same time, the government has gradually been privatizing some state-owned enterprises. The position and role of private business (as limited liability, joint-stock, joint venture firm, individual household, and so on) became more important in the services and goods production economy of Vietnam, to spur economic growth and integration with overseas markets.

The legal environment for commerce has been consolidated under the law. Vietnam's business executives are hardworking, dynamic and intelligent. They need assistance in capital and technology to compete against imported goods. On the other hand, the trade information environment has been improved. Social infrastructure, including transportation and telecommunications, has been upgraded.

Apart from state support, Vietnam's private business should have assistance and co-operation from foreign partners on the basis of mutual benefits if business expansion is desired. With an Australian partnership on such a basis, the long-term interests of Vietnamese and Australian businesses will be assured.

13 Public Administration in Vietnam

0 7 7
P 3 5
J 4 5   D 7 3

Nguyen Anh Tuan and Tran Van Hoa

GENERAL INTRODUCTION

The field of administration is a large one. The information in this chapter relates only to the principal field, the three aspects of administrative operation: law, the administrative machinery and personnel or cadres.

The Situation Before 1986

Before the economic reforms of 1986, when a centrally-planned economy was strictly in force in Vietnam, an administrative structure had taken shape and was, in fact, in operation in a relatively stable form. However, the functions and tasks of this early structure were not yet clear or concrete.

Law

During the period before 1986, legal codes and rules were not sufficiently formulated to direct institutions to operate in accordance with their functional task. This task was to have qualified specialists who could clearly define their work towards the Citizens' Act and actions for the good of a socialist country.

From 1960 to 1985, the number of promulgated laws in Vietnam consisted of only twenty-five Acts – that is, on average one Act was promulgated each year. The general laws and rules affecting every citizen in the country existed only to some extent in the Constitution and legal codes, and these were concerned only with fundamental areas. We can therefore say that, in the management of socioeconomic activities by state institutions and individuals, the administrative operation in Vietnam at that time did not exactly follow the law and the Constitution.

Administrative Machinery

Before 1986, the administrative machinery was still cumbersome and its functions were not clearly defined. In the high-level administrative divisions in the provinces and their branches, there was no distinction between the functions of economic management and state management units. At commune and district levels, the administrative machinery was usually limited to management, with a focus essentially on clarifying administrative procedures and settling social disputes. It was not interested in other problems of the citizen as correctly demanded by a proper public administration. The main causes of this situation are as follows:

- At both macro and micro levels, a knowledge of the state administrative management was not common and the management itself was not implemented in accordance with its objectives.
- There was an overlap or repetition of management in settling many socioeconomic problems and citizens' other activities.
- At a low administrative level (that is, in the communes), it was often the case that the state divisions or units executed a function for which they did not have management responsibility.

Civil Servants

Before 1986, the majority of state administrative and management officers at all levels in Vietnam were not adequately trained in their professional occupation. A proper job specification order and a training programme of the cadres or functionaries were only implemented after President Ho Chi Minh signed the Decree on Functionaries on 20 May 1950. A short time after that, because of the outbreak of war in the country, the training programme was discontinued. As a result, the main management of the different jobs in the state organizations and institutions was implemented by simply referring to the officers' standing orders. These officers were the regular staff of the state and had salary grades from junior staff members (Grade 1) to middle-ranking staff members (Grade 1).

An officer who was appointed through voting, recruitment, promotion, or assignment after graduation was recruited into the Communist Party, state organizations, businesses, and the armed forces. These officers were, as a rule, moved from assignment to assignment and from location to location during their working life. At their assigned branches and localities, few of these officers had a thorough knowledge of their professional occupation, or were experienced enough in their field of administration. In fact, the difference between the professional officers' training and experience was negligible.

Government Offices

Government offices, from central government to local state administrative organizations serving the public, were set up on a wide scale, but at the lower-ranking level of administration, the offices and other working facilities were still inadequate and the function of the officers was concentrated only on daily routine affairs. The result of this was that the officers were unable to keep in close touch with the public.

In summary, before 1986, many operations of a socioeconomic nature, including the state administrative operation in Vietnam, were dictated by many restrictive factors. This is understandable since, at that time, the aim of the whole of society was the liberation of the country. A result of this is that, for a number of years, all administrative and socioeconomic operations served this objective. This focus necessarily neglected other socioeconomic problems that had arisen in the country, and, worse still, requests for a regular administrative operation were often ignored. The public had to accept this kind of management, believing that it was for the good of the country. One has to admit, however, that at that period in the development of Vietnam the country's administrative operations and management did achieve their purposes: social stability and an active contribution to the implementation of the country's liberation objective.

The Period from 1986 to the late 1990s

After 1986, all socioeconomic operations, including administrative management, in Vietnam were gradually moved from a wartime economy to a more liberal one. The priority than became the renovation of the country, which moved gradually from the field of economic management to national administration.

Economic renovation required a succession of administrative renovations, first of all in the field of law. With the objective of building up Vietnam as a rich, strong, fair and civilized society, all areas of administrative operation, such as the administrative machinery, cadres, and government offices were reformed and renovated.

Constructing the Law System

In the renovation process, the legal framework is the area in which the government of Vietnam first wanted to see concrete results. From 1987 to 1995, the Vietnam government annually promulgated an average of eight to nine codes and laws, together with about ten ordinances and hundreds of decrees embracing all economic, political and social areas. Codes and laws had been designed to follow the policy of the Communist Party to redirect the emphasis and to establish a new attitude in government offices and state organizations, to work and live according to the law of the land. And the law covers all activities in all fields: citizens' activities, the political arena, and the social field. All this was intended to create working conditions for citizens in a sound social environment, encouraging individuals to show responsibility towards the community; and living and working within the spirit and letter, of the Constitution and the law.

At this time, the teaching of the laws to the general public was also strengthened. Knowledege of the law was introduced into the curriculum at primary and secondary schools. Legal codes and laws were proclaimed in the mass media. The activities of the education campaign included: organizing law workshops at a basic level for all strata of the public, developing the state and social organizations, establishing a control system to supervise the execution of the law by the state organs and authorized individuals, and establishing Economic Courts, Administrative Courts, and Labour Courts.

Administrative Machinery

The determination of the general direction, the principle of directing and reorganizing the administrative machinery and the operation statute of the administrative system are as follows:

- The government and administrative organizations at all levels must concentrate essentially on the state management of the economic, cultural, social and security areas; implement foreign policy in accordance with the stipulation of the law, and not intervene in the trading and production management of the country's economic units and business.
- At all levels, economic units will not participate in the state administrative management.
- Unifying the management of the branches and territories, defining clearly the competence and responsibility of all state administrative levels, and for the first time, setting up planning and budgets.
- Defining clearly the responsibility of the collective body or individuals in all operations, giving prominence to personal responsibility of the head of the unit in management.

- Many new organizations or units specializing in social affairs and management were formed; and some units whose regular staff needed to adopt a simple and effective attitude to carrying out their jobs were reorganized.
- Implementing the proper personal attention in the management in all fields of production, consumption, trade and residence to assure the social life of the public. Transferring social organizations and private individuals to state owned businesses to implement the management of public services. In this case, the government plays only a general supporting role.

Fostering and Strengthening the Officer Contingent

This is a stage that is experiencing active change. Administrative management officers at all levels, especially in the provinces and branches, gradually adapt their professional ability to meet the demand of the state management and the socioeconomic management units in the market economy. In 1995, the government opened ninety courses to improve the professional ability of the state administrative management staff. At that time, a number of officers were assigned further tasks on social affairs and management.

DEVELOPMENT DEMAND AND FORECASTS TO 2010

Though the country has had relative successes in its renovation process in all fields of administrative reform, the socioeconomic renovation and its progress are creating new demands and opportunities:

The Law

While a great number of codes and laws have been made, their content remained only at the principle or concept stage. Decrees, detailed regulations to implement the law, and guiding circulars are still lacking or were promulgated late. There are many cases in which a law was promulgated a year previously but it has not yet had any guiding decrees or circulars attached to facilitate its implementation. It is clear that there is an urgent need to have documents and stipulations to guide the execution of the law in Vietnam.

It is also often the case that new codes and laws are promulgated and they are executed at the same time as the old laws, with both laws lack guiding decrees or circulars. This has created a situation in which a law is interpreted differently in two different locations, or in two different branches in the same location. To avoid this type of contradiction or confusion in implementing the law, official guiding documents are urgently required by the administrative cadres and the people interested in the law in Vietnam in order to apply or interpret the law in a uniform manner throughout the country. Making these changes will create a better climate to help promote the country's socioeconomic renovation.

From the above-mentioned observations, the demands for public administration reform to be met are as follows:

● During the process of drafting the law, it is necessary that accompanying decrees and circulars guiding the execution of the law are drafted at the same time. This would complete the drafting process and overcome the problem of lacking documents to implement the law correctly.

● Setting up an official mechanism to control the legal and constitutional character of the juridical acts.

● Setting up an official mechanism to consider and determine the implications of the law before legal acts and stipulations are promulgated. This applies especially to legal acts promulgated by the government, its ministries and authorized provincial authorities.

● Defining the demarcation line of authority between the legislative, executive and judicial bodies.

- Regularly analyzing the effects and implications of the law by assessing public opinion and seeking advice from experts in the area affected by the law.
- Assuring that the content and quality of the legal system are appropriate for application in the new situation of socioeconomic renovation.

Machinery

The process of renovation of the legal and administrative institutions in the country necessarily raises the problem of how to strengthen the effectiveness of the operation by the administrative machinery, which aims at implementing two basic functions of the state organizations: (i) rule; and (ii) dictatorship in serving the people. To realize the above two functions, the administrative machinery at all levels of operation has to address the following issues:

- The central government and local authorities should concentrate on the management of macro- and microeconomic policy. This includes setting down a development strategy, formulating policy, making laws, and assuring political stability and national security.
- Taking care of the effects of sociocultural development, ensuring environmental protection, and protection against social evils as perceived by the law.
- Organizing the government machinery and administrative organizations, defining clearly the responsibility and authority of every organization and administrative rank, and overcoming the overlapping of responsibility and authority between organizations and administrative ranks.

Personnel

Renovation in general, and administrative and economic renovations in particular, must have an officer contingent to carry out the execution of the law to meet all practical demands that accompany the renovations. The problem that arises from this requirement is:

- The officer contingent at the time of writing still lacks the necessary qualifications regarding professional ability, fluency in foreign languages, and other required knowledge.

At the beginning of 1993, the government started to standardize its systems by introducing different grades for administrative staff. The composition of the administrative staff was as follows: 30 per cent in the central and ministerial divisions; and 60–70 per cent in the local division. The local division staff do not have sufficient qualifications to be included in the central and ministeral divisions.

- In central administration, judges are appointed by the state president. Thirty per cent of provincial judges and 50 per cent of district judges do not have sufficient professional qualifications.
- The standard of foreign languages among the administrative officers who require it for their jobs is still inadequate. In 1994, an investigation on foreign-language proficiency for administrative officers resulted in: 61 per cent of the middle and high-ranking officials spoke a foreign language and their standards were as follows: 16.89 per cent Level A; 15.6 per cent Level B; 25.53 per cent Level C; and 2.94 per cent at high-school level.
- Administrative officers at the basic level (that is, the commune or quarter) are of a low cultural standard. The People's Council delegates of the communes and quarters during the session 1994–5 were of the following standards: Cultural standard Grades 1 and 2: 92.40 per cent; of which: Grade 1; 43.56 per cent; and Grade 2; 48.84 per cent.
- The mentoring and training work should be continued for administrative officers as a result of the demand for

practical administrative management of branch or division officers and for an acceptable standard among all ranks.

- A limitation of the system: training and its use is separated from each other.
- Unavailability of retraining guidelines: training bases are scattered around the country and continue to be divided regarding the sharing of infrastructure and resources.
- There is a seriously insufficient number of teachers. Schools are assured of only 30 per cent of necessarily qualified teachers at training schools.
- The training programmes are still inadequate and are based on the training objectives of previous years. Teaching documents and lecture notes are inadequate.
- From the above-mentioned problems in the field of public administration, these points need to be addressed urgently:
- Timely promoting professional qualifications and equipping management officers of all levels and ranks and other experts in the field with a good knowledge on the State administrative management. To have a sufficient professional standard for all administrative officers in the immediate future, the government should formulate and announce regulations on the responsibility of administrative officers before they take up their positions.
- Officers in some new branches of administration, fields of social affairs, and management, should be basically trained and immediately provided with all necessary general knowledge on administration.
- Programmes to raise the cultural standards and professional ability knowledge of the functionary, particularly the functionary at the basic level of administration.
- Strengthening and perfecting a training programme for administrative officers.

EXISTING PLANS

Socioeconomic Development and Stabilization Strategy to the year 2000

The following development and stabilization strategy has been formulated: for the state administration machinery and staff to 2000:

- Reconstructing the organizational structure and operational mechanism of the state administration machinery, and having a qualified officer contingent. The reform's main objective is aimed at constructing a state administrative system, from central to basic, that has sufficient authority and, capacity:
- Having qualified officers to implement the state management function nationwide.
- State administration organization at all levels is based on a unified system of the law and policy, in accordance with the state plan, to implement the state management function in all socioeconomic activities and by all organisations and individuals in the country. This unified system also assures a serious execution of the law, pays attention to people's living conditions, supports the local socioeconomic infrastructure, and reinforces national security and defence.
- Cutting down on red tape at all administrative management levels, from the central to the basic, and simplifying the administrative function and machinery, especially at the district level.
- Reforming the organizational and operational statute of the government offices of all categories, cancelling unnecessary intermediary links, simplifying employment conditions of regular staff, reforming administrative procedures, and gradually modernizing administrative techniques.
- Retraining administrative personnel in line with the reformed administrative mechanism.

- Defining clearly all offices to be elected in accordance with the terms and conditions of the appointment.
- Formulating the functionary statute in every field of state management operation aimed at forming a skilful, qualified and high-quality professional officer contingent within the law.

During the five years 1991–5, the programme was developed with significiant content as follows:

- Amending the Constitution, strengthening the socialist legal system, and continuing to amend and expand the system of law.
- Raising the standard of state organizations consistent with the law reforms, early promulgation of the law, organizing the implementation of the law, and assuring state management to improve the country's social conditions.
- Educating people about the law.
- Reorganizing administrative offices and their regular staff from 1991 onwards to make the state machinery lighter and more effective in operation.
- Establishing a staff contingent of good political quality, a sense of responsibility, and skilled in applying their professional knowledge.

Plan for the Period 1996–2000

The following items are in the plan for public administration reforms in Vietnam for the period 1996–2000. They express more forcefully the demand for administrative reforms, including the areas of legislation formulation, law supervision, law implementation, and reforming administrative institutions.

- Continuing to build up a legal system consistent with the free market mechanism and compatible with socialist characteristics. Promulgating new laws: Commercial Law, Banking Law, Customs Law, Post and Telecommunications Law, Electricity Power Law, Construction Law, Technological Science Law, and Water Resources Law.

- Amending the current laws and ordinances on tax, home ownership, foreign investment, and company and private business.
- Improving the promulgation of legal documents assuring a united charter on the content, the commencement of operation, and the effect of law execution.
- Issuing the promulgation and proclamation of the legal acts at the same time as the required amended administrative procedures to implement them.
- Developing a strong education campaign about the new laws promulgated.
- Reorganizing the administrative machinery, in both central and local administrations.
- Making concrete the state management devolution between the government organizations and municipality administration levels directly under the central administration.
- Promulgating the statute of civil servants and their functions, and indicating the need for using open examinations when recruiting staff or nominating people for official positions.
- Faster training of a younger staff contingent to implement plans to improve the standard of public administration.

Forecasting Action Plans in Public Administration Reforms

Law

For the period up to the year 2010, the work of legal experts in the country must concentrate on drafting and promulgating decrees and circulars to guide the implementation of the promulgated laws and codes, assuring at the same time the uniform character of the codes and their appropriate application in all branches and localities.

- Amending some articles to be consistent with socio-economic changes, particularly those articles that are related to the renovation process, the implementation of an 'open-door' policy and the motto: 'Vietnamese people would like to be friends with the peoples of all countries'. Popularizing the law by publication and by other mass media, and exhorting all State organizations and the public to work and live by the law.

Administrative Machinery

Assuring the effectiveness of the administrative machinery in its functions of ruling and serving the people. Promoting the attitude, the spirit and the quality of services rendered to the people in accordance with the legal stipulation on the function and task of the central organizations in the state administrative machinery.

- Improving working conditions, facilities and equipment, modernizing them first in the high-ranking government offices and gradually to lower levels.

Personnel

- Developing strong supplemental or in-service training and retraining programmes.
- Implementing the guidelines for both civil servants and their functions.
- Standardizing civil servants and their activities.

IMPLEMENTING CONDITIONS

Home Conditions

- The socioeconomic situation continues to be stable and to develop strongly (as at November 1995, the average economic growth attained was 8 per cent per year). Estimated economic growth in the period 1996–2000 is 9–10 per cent per year. Because of the impact of the Asian currency crisis during the financial year 1997/8, however, the projected growth rate for Vietnam may be less than the above rate.

- There is unanimous approbation inside the Communist Party, the state, and the government, who undertaking to implement the administrative operation reform by producing annual or five-year action plans.
- The development of complete socioeconomic programmes and the need for deeper and wider administrative reforms.
- Retraining programmes have been developed in the country and since 1995 they have been developed especially for the functionary.

Overseas conditions

Many international organizations have supported, and are supporting, the implementation of the administrative reforms in Vietnam. Some of this support is listed below for reference:

- Project VIE 92-002 of the United Nations Development Programme supports administrative reform in Vietnam.
- The Canadian Law Association works with the Legal Committee of Vietnam's National Assembly on administrative reform.
- A number of seminars have been organized to discuss issues of administrative reform in Vietnam. One of them is the seminar on Commercial Law, and drafting the Law on Administrative Reform.
- The collaboration between Vietnam and the Federal Republic of Germany to organize a seminar on Technical Assistance for Administrative Reform.

14 Science-Technology in Vietnam

Kim Van Chinh

REAL SITUATIONS OF SCIENCE-TECHNOLOGY

Science-Technology Developments in the Period 1945–85

The greatest and most embraced characteristic influencing the formation and development of the techno-scientific fields in the period 1945–85 was that the objective and solutions implementing the development of science-technology were connected with the strategic objectives of the revolution for national liberation. However, since 1954, when the North restored and developed the economy, and since 1975, when the country was reunified, one of the objectives of science-technology has been to contribute to the serving of economic development.

Up to the period 1975–86, the whole country concentrated its efforts on the construction of a techno-material basis of socialism, on the grounds that it still faced a frontier war and the risk of a greater war.

The overall objectives, position and role of science-technology in this period was clearly determined. But when defining concrete objectives and organization, and the developments and solutions for branches (regional localities) in the science-technology field, it did not define the main point of development, the preferential objective, practical and effective solutions. The organization for developing science-technology based on the concentrated, bureaucratic and subsidized mode in the period had led to big differences in practical organizations, spreading investment and so on. (In only five years, 1981–5, seventy-six tech-scientific programmes of national significance had been developed).

137

A noteworthy thing in science-technology development during this period was the loss of balance in the structure of the science-technology field. In practice, the social science aspect developed very slowly and was deficient when compared with practical demands, with international standards and natural science development. Science-technology also developed slowly, and was biased compared with basic research.

SCIENCE-TECHNOLOGY DEVELOPMENT FROM 1986 UP TO THE LATE 1990s

The period from 1986 up to the time of writing has been characterized by the transformation of the economy into a market mechanism together with the expansion of international co-operation in economics and science-technology. The change in the management mechanism has brought about basic changes in organizations, financial issues and product sales and purchases, emphasizing the field of science-technology.

For that reason, science-technological development in this period had a pioneering character in the majority of fields. But it also had many changes in development objectives towards some fields, especially basic research fields. Though in need of much state financial assistance, it was ordered never the less to streamline its request for financial assistance.

In Fundamental Science and Techniques

Science-technology experts have carried out much fundamental research in the fields of mathematics, informatics, physics, chemistry, biology and science in general. The results were very noticeable: about 1600 documents and scientific reports have been published in science magazines and journals in Vietnam and at international conferences, of which 500 were of high quality.

Human Culture and Social Science

Since 1986 this area has been developed by leaps and bounds through the impact of the party and the state's renovation policy. With the renovation spirit, social science thinking has changed the research emphasis from a scholastic approach biased towards the ideological system to basic research and applications. Noticeable achievements were as follows.

- Completing ten research programmes (from KX-01 to KX-10) on Human Culture and Social Science. The essential contribution was to return to a clear perception on the way to reconstruct the country following the socialist orientation and the orientations of socio-economic development; to contribute to the renovating and perfecting of the economic management mechanism to suppress inflation; to maintain the stabilization process; to construct scientific arguments for social policies; and to create a new image for society.
- Collecting numerous Han-Nom documents and ancient books with a cultural legacy of the ethnic people.
- Carrying out a series of practical investigations and surveys to support basic research and to formulate policy.

APPRAISING THE REAL SITUATION OF SCIENCE-TECHNOLOGY

In general, science-technology in Vietnam made great advances during the period of the country's construction and defence (1945–96), but the contributions of science-technology were not emphasized, and their role was not brought adequately into play during that time. Science-technology achievements were not great, and while the application of domestic and foreign technological progress was limited and incomplete these was a weakness in capacity, quality and production, leading to a backward situation in economic development. Science-technology did not produce any goods at this time, because the science-technology market had not yet taken shape, nor had the conditions on the property rights been formulated. So, generally, the standard of Vietnamese science-technology is very low (production equipment and research equipment were lagging by up to 2–4 generations, pollution caused by the technology in use was high, and with high coefficient of raw material amortization, low labour capacity, and so on). The potential of science-technology is still weak at the time of writing, and still, not meeting the country's development demands for industrialization and modernization.

The science-technology officer contingent is still insufficient, in quality and quantity, and in the structure of branches and trades. In the whole country, there are about 4 million technical workers, of whom over 1.2 million are of the middle-ranking class, 800 000 are from high-education cadres, and about 10 000 are from postgraduate cadres, which is equal to 1.2 per cent of all graduate cadres. In colleges and institutions, this rate reaches 10.4 per cent (in developed countries the rate is 25–30 per cent). The proportion of researchers in the population is 350 per one million people. This rate is not low but the number of people working in science-technology offices has had a tendency to decrease gradually. Moreover, the standard structure in research agencies or institutions is not complete: the rates of high-ranking officers and technical workers are low (10.4 per cent and 3 per cent, respectively), and the average age for this group is high (40–45 years old). This leads to the risk of ageing of the science-technology officers in the branches, and is not consistent with development demand. The officers were generally concentrated in some natural basic science branches, resulting in other branches suffering a lack of skills, technological applications and development possibilities (the officers at science-technology branches made up only 15.4 per cent of the total number). While the knowledge potential of individual scientific officers is good, it lacks the element of community co-operation, making Vietnam a country having very few strong science-technology collective units.

The system of education and training given to weak science-technology officers is biased by the teaching of theory, and seriously lacking in modern equipment and the capacity to spread practical skills and the development of creative thinking to students.

Technology used in the national economy is in general lagging behind by several generations when compared with the advanced standards in the rest of the world (except in some special branches such as Post and Telecommunications). Technologies freshly imported in recent years were in most of the cases obsolete (an investigation at forty-two companies newly importing technologies shows that 76 per cent of the machines were manufactured in the years 1950–60; 50 per cent of freshly imported machines were reconditioned; and 70 per cent of the machinery had outlived their depreciation period in the overseas countries).

FORECASTING VIETNAM'S SCIENCE-TECHNOLOGY DEVELOPMENT DEMAND TO 2010

Essential Directions of Science-Technology Demand to 2010

- Building up a strong scientific base to support the decision process at branches, levels, and the adoption of a sound theoretical system underlying the strategy of industrialization and modernization.
- Strengthening the application of science-technology achievements and advanced environment protection to speed up the renovation process and to raise technological standards in essential production and service branches.
- Raising the capacity to study and develop within Vietnam, using science-technology potential.
- Constructing a manpower source capable of approaching international technology standards; selecting, adapting and controlling imported technologies;

transforming and modernizing traditional technologies; capable of falling in line with international standards and at least in some selected fields; and able to create its own special technologies.

- In the operation of scientific research, the study, application and absorption of technology is the main purpose, but to reserve a certain part of the operation to basic research may also be necessary to satisfy the technological development demand.

- Preferably using the latest knowledge, high technology (particularly automation technology) at the decisive links with the intention of raising capacity and product quality. Four high-technology fields that need attention are: information technology; biological technology; material technology; and automated fabrication technology, as well as some programmes related to infrastructure construction such as energy, transport-communications, and resources management. Additionally, there remain programmes having a public character such as the environment, medical problems, agriculture and so on.

- Preferably investing in the construction of science-technology organizations, reserving a budget for training techno-scientific officers in accordance with preferential technology directions.

- Studying to promulgate necessary legal documents for science-technology operations (Law on Science-Technology, Law on Property Rights, and necessary laws for the science-technological market to be developed).

CONDITIONS TO IMPLEMENT THE SCIENCE-TECHNOLOGY DEVELOPMENT STRATEGY

Constructing a Science-Technology Officer Contingent

Reforming the science-technology training system to enable it to train people to make and use science-technology in the twenty-first century, and implementing, at the same time, a series of concerted measures so that the science-technology officer contingent can be developed.

Financial Investment in Science-Technology

The financial level of investment for science-technology over the years must be raised in both relative and absolute terms in budgetary expenditure and GDP (the present level of under 1 per cent of the budgetary expenditure in Vietnam at the time of writing is too low. It is fifty times lower than the world average level).

In the coming years, the above situation has to be overcome by increasing the investment level, encouraging the connection of science-technology with production, and mobilizing other non-budgetary investment capital sources.

Constructing the System of Organs Operating on Science-Technology

In the coming years, the basic construction investment fund for science-technology will have to be increased greatly in accordance with the development plan and objectives of the country. In the organization of science-technology institutions, it has to implement the plan to merge the colleges with the National Scientific Centres, and to connect research institutions with production in order to construct gradually science-technology collective units of a high standard, and strong in organizational and operative experience.

Constructing a Legal System of Science-Technology

Early promulgation of the law on science-technology and related legal acts is required. Perfecting legal acts on the protection of the ownership of knowledge, on technological transfer, and on civil contract regimes in science-technology operations to conform with the civil code is also required. It is necessary to introduce policies and measures encouraging science-technology operations to renovate production technology as implied in the relevant articles in the socioeconomic law and policy of the government.

Increasing the Activity of Techno-Scientific Associations

Implementing policies to encourage economics and to assure their judicial character so that the techno-scientific associations can implement their social function towards the formation of policies, socioeconomic development planning, and science-technology development. Entrusting the techno-scientific associations with organizing techno-scientific competitions, considering ways to award excellent scientific research works, to organize scientific seminars, and to disseminate scientific knowledge. These associations are permitted to found research organs and science-technology consulting services, and to produce scientific products according to legal stipulation.

Developing International Co-operation in Science-Technology

International co-operation in science-technology has to be combined with economic co-operation in order to import a series of appropriate advanced technologies to serve the industrialization and modernization of the country. A certain part of foreign-assisted capital funding must be reserved for training/retraining of science-technology officers and management officers, particularly young officers. Close monitoring of the reports of the delegations going abroad for study tours at state expense must be undertaken so that many individuals can refer to it and use it profitably in the future.

CAPABILITY TO ATTRACT FOREIGN INVESTMENT IN SCIENCE-TECHNOLOGY

By the year 2010, the demand for foreign investment will be great in science-technology, estimated at about

25–30 per cent of operating expenses, and concentrated in the following fields:

- Training and retraining the science-technology officer contingent, essentially higher education and postgraduate training in the preferred fields (information technology, biological technology, materials technology, automation, and some branches in which Vietnam has not yet achieved a good training base). In these fields, it essentially develops the ODA source of funds, including non-refunding aid and refunding aid following the intergovernmental co-operation programme. Additionally, non-governmental financial assistance will also be developed in the training of science-technology officers at higher education and postgraduate levels.
- In the educational field, projects of educational system reform from primary education to higher education (sponsored by the World Bank and the UNDP); some technical support projects to raise training capacity at some big training bases; joint-venture projects on the basics of foreign equipment; the use of Vietnamese science-technology officers to study technological developments; the fabrication of some science-technology products; or implementing necessary science-technology services, and so on, are most desirable.
- Receiving and exploiting some necessary equipment to serve measurement standards, diagnosis and disease treatment, professional use of scientific equipment of branches (in the past, this direction was well developed in co-operative relations with the Netherlands, Sweden and France). Following this direction, the essential form of co-operation is the ODA aid and direct co-operation between science-technology organizations and foreign science-technology operation funds.
- Co-operation, the exchange of science-technology information in which, the Vietnamese side is essentially assisted (in many forms) to gain facilities and

skills to update world science-technology information, and introduce gradually its science-technology products and information to the world.

- Thus, it can be realized that, in the science-technology field, the form of FDI (including joint ventures and 100 per cent foreign-owned capital) can develop very slowly and the essential forms are therefore aid or co-operation in research and training. In the future, this tendency will continue to develop.

In recent years, financial assistance and research co-operation from CIS and other East European countries, has declined sharply because of socioeconomic–political changes in these countries, while financial assistance and research co-operation with capitalist countries and international organizations have increased rapidly.

Countries having strong relations with Vietnam in this field are:

- The Netherlands. Concentrating on the fields of agriculture, irrigation, industry and state management (annually: 10–15 scholarships for long-term training; short-term courses; financial assistance with twenty-three projects for colleges with an average amount of US$0.2 million per project.
- Germany. Essentially issuing scholarships from scientific funds to science-technology institutions.
- Sweden. Co-operation is mainly channelled through two state organs of Sweden, concentrating on the medical field, measurements, and foundation treatment in construction (the total sum sponsored to projects is US$3.5 million in equipment and 200 training places).
- France. Essentially concentrated in the co-operative fields of agriculture, medicine, biology, applied mathematics, informatics, science-technology information exchange, training (over fifty research projects have been sponsored, supplying many documents, equipment and scientific facilities, and opening two centres

– a French language training centre and an economic management training centre).

Other countries supporting science-technology co-operation are: Australia, Canada, the USA and so on; co-operation is also developing in the fields of training and small projects.

A noticeable financial assistance source for science-technology operations comes from international organizations such as the UNDP, FAO, UNESCO, WIPO, and non-governmental organizations of the other countries in the region and the rest of the world. The UNDP alone, in four successive fiscal years from 1977 to 1996, assisted financially, with a total of about US$100 million. This made up 50 per cent of total financial assistance to Vietnam. The purpose of the assistance was to equip modern technical facilities in science-technological bases and also to restore some industrial production bases. Science-technology projects which enjoy financial assistance from international organizations are of the scale of US$200 000 to US$2 million.

15 Vietnam's Tourism

Vu Tuan Canh

£83

INTRODUCTION

The Potential of Vietnam's Tourism

Vietnam is situated on the eastern side of the Indo-Chinese peninsula with its north–south length of 1700 km and narrowing in its central zone to a maximum width of 50 km. It borders China in the north, Laos and Cambodia in the west, and the East Sea in the east and the south, with a total coastal length of 3260 km. It is a tropical country with two distinguishable seasons: hot and cold.

The country has a diverse topography, sloping down gradually from west to east. This offers a great advantage for tourism development, as there are attractive places and holiday resorts for domestic and overseas tourists in the mountains, the midlands and the delta regions. There are numerous beautiful beaches and many islands and bays of natural beauty, such as Ha Long bay.

The population of Vietnam was 76 million people in 1996, living mostly in the delta of the Red River, the Mekong River, and the central coastal zone. Vietnam has four main economic axes: Hanoi–Hai Phong–Quang Ninh in the north, Da Nang–Hue in the central area, Nha Trang–Da Lat in the central south, and Ho Chi Minh City–Vung Tau in the south. Apart from the advantageous conditions of its topography and climate, and the abundance and diversity of animals and plants, Vietnam also has a special culture with a 4000-year history. The country has sixty ethnic groups with separate cultural features and traditional architecture with national colours reflecting the different development periods of the country's history. Those features are distributed in a number of areas, forming typical tourist environments, which are located near large cities and important international frontier passes to facilitate travel and accommodation. In the future, the Indo-Chinese Tourism Route (Vietnam–Laos–Cambodia) will be an important route in the international tourism itinerary in South East Asia.

THE CONDITION OF VIETNAM'S TOURISM IN RECENT YEARS

Vietnam's new open-door economic policy has encouraged a strong development of its tourism industry in recent years. Prior to 1989, Vietnam's tourism industry was undeveloped, but since 1990, it has been expanded and has integrated itself gradually into the progress of the region.

In the period 1986–9, the number of international visitors coming to Vietnam is as follows. In 1986, Vietnam received 54.5 thousand visitors from abroad; in 1987, 73.3 thousand; in 1988, 10.4 thousand; and in 1989, 187.6 thousand. They came mainly from the former USSR and Eastern European countries, as well as Vietnamese living and working abroad. The growth rate of visitors coming to Vietnam from 1990 to 1996 has greatly increased. In 1990, Vietnam received 250 thousand international visitors; in 1991, 300 thousand; in 1992, 440 thousand; in 1993, 670 thousand; in 1994, one million; in 1995, 1.35 million; and in 1996, about 1.6 million. During 1990–6, the visitors were mainly from Taiwan, Japan, Hong Kong and France.

In addition to overseas visitors, the number of domestic tourists has also increased regularly. In 1991, the number was one million; in 1995, it was 5.5 million; and in 1996, about 7 million. When compared with the period 1986–9, visitors in the period 1990–6 have increased in both quantity and quality.

Hotels and guest-houses have been developed constantly, in quantity as well as in quality. There were in the whole country in June 1996 over 3050, with 51 000 rooms available, of which 27 000 rooms (53 per cent) reach international standards. A range of high-quality hotels has been developed throughout the country. There has been a continuous improvement in guidelines and policies on tourism approved by the General Department of Tourism, to expand the industry. An ordinance on tourism was submitted for the government's approval late in 1996. Twenty-two provinces and cities in the whole country have had their tourism planning approved. The international relationship of Vietnam tourism continues to be raised. The country maintained contractual relations with more than 800 tourist firms in the world in 1996, compared to 500 firms in 1995. Other services such as information, internal affairs, customs and air transport have also been improved.

Foreign investment in Vietnam's tourism industry has increased remarkably in recent years. From 1988–94, 129 projects were licenced, of which there were 117 joint-venture projects; five projects of 100 per cent foreign capital; and seven 'business co-operation contract' co-operative projects.

Among 129 licenced projects, licences of ten projects have been revoked, and the remaining 119 have a total registered capital of US$2 billion; legal capital of US$1.5 billion; 69 per cent of capital contributed by foreign parties; and 31 per cent by Vietnamese parties. Twelve 5-star hotels with 2800 rooms; twenty-six 4-star hotels with 5400 rooms; and forty-six 3-star hotels with 5200 rooms have been built. Thirty per cent of the projects had been put into operation by 1994, and by 1996 the number of projects had increased to 160, with a total registered capital of more than US$4 billion invested in the fields of tourism and hotels. In 1996 there were throughout the country 14 000 hotel rooms, several golf courses, and a number of entertainment bases operating. By the end of October 1994, the country had 1713 tourist business organizations, of which most were in the accommodation business (1572 organizations). The key areas are: Hanoi, with 226 organizations; Ho Chi Minh City, with 352; Thanh Hoa, with 152; and Lam Dong, with 293.

In 1993, revenue from tourism provided 2.8 per cent of the country's GDP, and would be 5.8 per cent if the revenue from the other branches related to tourism was included. It has been predicted that, by the year 2000, revenue from tourism will be 5 per cent of GDP, and 10 per cent of GDP in 2010. It is possible to say that, in recent years, Vietnam's tourism has achieved good results, but it also has many constraints. In order to catch up with the development speed of other branches, as well as other countries, its weaknesses must be recognized and necessary measures taken to overcome them.

THE CONSTRAINTS OF VIETNAM'S TOURISM

Activities of Vietnam Tourism during past years have not been maximizing its available potential. Its business and services have not been sufficiently diverse and of high quality, exposing weak competitiveness. Staff with high professional skills and fluent in foreign languages are in short supply. Infrastructure for tourist resorts and supporting facilities are insufficient. The protection of the tourist environment has not been paid due attention, and the coordination between branches, while achieving some progress, has not really been synchronous. These problems should be resolved quickly to facilitate Vietnam's tourism development.

Apart from these problems, the renovation and reformation of administrative procedures to create a favourable environment for tourists are also important. In fact, in recent years, these problems have sometimes hindered tourism's development. The greatest problem recently has been the imbalance between the supply of and demand for rooms and beds in hotels: they have increased more rapidly than the increase in the number of tourists. Furthermore, it is common that hotels in some localities are small and of poor quality, with their prices not corresponding to the service quality, so that the number of guests is few and there are many vacancies. Among the 3050 accommodation facilities with 51 000 rooms in total, only 53 per cent are good enough to attract foreign visitors. And they are distributed unevenly, leading to temporary local surpluses and shortages at the same time. The mini-hotels are also less effective because of their weaknesses relating to equipment and entertainment facilities, and poor structural features.

The tourism service has not created a stable base to attract tourists, and still lacks representative offices abroad to advertise and develop the scope of its activities. Opportunities have been missed to attract foreign tourists to Vietnam because they have not been given information about Vietnam's changes in policy. The efficiency of tourist activities in some locations is still low because these activities are based on a 'hurry up' or 'instant' design without a concrete programme or long-term plan. Currently, tourist activities are concentrated mainly on the exploitation of such services as catering, accommodation and travelling. Entertainment services have not been exploited and have no power to attract the tourists for long stays and return visits, for example. These weaknesses of Vietnam's tourism can be overcome, provided that there are appropriate guidelines, solutions and strategic planning for immediate and long-term developments.

THE STRATEGIC ORIENTATION FOR VIETNAM TOURISM TO 2000 AND 2010

The main objectives decided by the Vietnam government regarding its overall planning and development of tourism to the year 2000, and to 2010 are shown below.

Main Objectives

Economic objectives To optimize the contribution of tourism to the national revenue, and to solve job problems for the workforce.

Environmental objectives To develop tourism in tandem with the protection of the ecological environment, the social environment, and the preservation of natural relics and national cultural values.

Social objectives To use the experience of tourism development in other countries, and at the same time ensure a positive social effectiveness by means of the diversification and improvement of tourism products and service quality. Together with the development of international tourism, the development of tourism in Vietnam must be emphasized to facilitate a cultural circulation between localities and ethnic groups in the country.

Quantitative goals These are shown in Table 15.1.

Table 15.1   The quantitative goals of Vietnam's tourist industry

Year	Quantity of foreign visitors (millions people)	Revenue from international tourism not including transportation (US$ billions)	Quantity of domestic visitors (millions people)	Ratio of revenue from tourism in GDP (per cent)	
1995	1.4	0.40	4.5	3.5	(7.2)*
2000	3.8	1.06	11.0	5.0	(9.0)
2010	8.7	8.000	25.0	10.0	(20.0)

Note: *The numbers in brackets ( ) include revenue from other services related to the tourist industry.

Tourism Organization

This focuses on planning and the exploitation of three main tourist zones:

- The northern tourist zone (Zone I). This zone comprises twenty-three provinces, from Ha Giang to Ha Tinh. Its centre is Hanoi. Hanoi–Hai Phong–Quang Ninh forms a triangle a force for driving growth.

Important tourist spots such as Hanoi and its vicinity, Ha Long Bay, Cat Ba, Do Son, Ba Be (Cao Bang), Dien Bien (Lai Chau) will be built in this zone.

- The northern central tourist zone (Zone II). This zone comprises five provinces, from Quang Binh to Quang Ngai. It has a lot of tourist potential not yet being exploited. The tourism in this zone is still a low priority compared with other branches. Its geographical position is advantageous, especially for connecting tours with Laos and Thailand. The key spots for tourism in this zone are the ancient royal capital of Hue and the port city of Da Nang.

- The southern central and southern tourist zone (Zone III). This zone is made up of twenty-five provinces and cities. Its centre is Ho Chi Minh City. Its driving force for growth is the Ho Chi Minh City–Nha Trang–Da Lat triangle. This is the most advantageous of the three zones, and forms of tourism that can be exploited are abundant. The zone has several beautiful beaches. The key areas that need to be developed are: Nha Trang, Lam Dong, Ba Ria, Vung Tau, Ho Chi Minh City and its vicinity, and areas such as Tay Ninh, Dong Nai, Con Dao, Phu Quoc, for example.

Continuing the Perfection and Renovation

There are four principal points in the renovation process: improving lawful instrument systems; strengthening the state management system from central to local authorities; the rearrangement of tourist business systems towards specialization; and environment management and tourism planning.

Tourism Development Strategies

Basic Strategies

- To create special tourist products bearing the national colours, especially cultural, historic, artistic traditions, habits and customs and so on, aiming at competing in and seizing the market.

- To create specialized tourist products such as tourism for improving health, sea-rest medical treatment, cave tourism, golf courses, cultural activities with national traditions, conference tourism, festivals and so on.
- Growth strategy by means of diversifying tourist products to meet the requirements of foreign and domestic tourists.
- Strategy on the preservation and protection of tourist relics; making plans to divide functional zones in large tourist areas to define the zones that need complete protection, the zones that are reserved for development, and reclaimed zones.
- Strategy for tourism investment. To encourage every form of domestic and foreign investment into tourism projects according to development planning. In addition to the law on investment, there is a need to have other instruments such as ordinances or laws on tourism.
- Regarding hotels. To focus on two groups of hotels: transit or temporary-stay hotels (1–3 stars) and de luxe hotels (4–5 stars). The number of extra transit hotel rooms that need to be built has been estimated as shown in Table 15.2.

Table 15.2   The number of extra transit hotel rooms that need to be built

Period	Zone I (rooms)	Zone II (rooms)	Zone III (rooms)	Whole country (rooms)	Total investment capital (US$ millions)
Up to the year 2000	5 900	1 400	8 915	16 200	1 200
From 2000 to 2010	151 000	3 350	24 100	42 660	2 668

The quantity of extra super hotel rooms that needs to be built has been estimated as shown in Table 15.3. Thus, up to the year 2000, Vietnam's tourism industry needs investment capital of about US$6.44 million for the construction of hotels. To reach this objective, the co-operation and assistance of foreign companies is very necessary for Vietnam.

Table 15.3   The number of de luxe hotel rooms needed

Period	Zone I (rooms)	Zone II (rooms)	Zone III (rooms)	Whole country (rooms)	Total investment capital (US$ millions)
Up to the year 2000	2 000	200	4 500	6 700	830
From 2000 to 2010	4 960	550	10 340	15 850	1 708

- The strategy of tourism staff training. Training and retraining aims at meeting the immediate and long-term demands for tourism staff of every form, in both the short and the long term, at home and abroad.
- Strategy of raising the quality of tourist products. To create special products for each tourist zone, joining with foreign countries, especially the countries in the region and neighbouring countries with a common border, to combine tours with them.
- Strategy of raising the quality of tourist services in several areas: service attitude, diversity, facilities of goods and services, and the willingness of the service.

Areas having the priority for investment in tourism development.

1. The capital, Hanoi, and its vicinity, to create resorts and weekend tourist areas for the capital.

2. Ha Long–Bai Tu Long–Cat Ba–Do Son (Quang Ninh–Hai Phong) have formed a group with great competitiveness in the region.
3. Hue–Da Nang–Lao Bao: to preserve and exploit cultural, architectural and natural relics; to develop tourist infrastructure; and to connect with tours to or from Laos and Thailand.
4. Nha Trang–Da Lat–Minh Chu: to build resorts combining marine environments and mountainous beauty spots, and to build the largest tourist area in Vietnam in Dai Lanh (Khanh Hoa).
5. Vung Tau–Long Hai–Con Dao: to create a weekend resort for Ho Chi Minh City.
6. Ho Chi Minh City and its vicinity: to develop a tourism project along the Mekong River to Phnom-Penh, Laos and Thailand, and to create a cultural village of ethnic groups in Ho Chi Minh City.

AUSTRALIA–VIETNAM CO-OPERATIVE PERSPECTIVES IN TOURISM

Up to the year 2000 and on to 2010, Vietnam will need a fairly large amount of capital to invest in the field of tourism. Together with the mobilization of capital resources within the country, Vietnam also plans to encourage foreign investment. Australia is a country with economic potential and wide experience in this field. During recent years, co-operation between the two countries in this field has achieved good results, especially in the hotel business. At the time of writing Australia is ranked third among countries that have invested in tourism in Vietnam, after Hong Kong and Taiwan. In the coming years, together with investment in building tourist products and projects, co-operation in training of tourist staff will also need special attention.

16 Transport-Communication in Vietnam

ICTC staff

INTRODUCTION

Starting from the status of a less developed economy, a prolonged war, and with a very complicated terrain, transport-communication in Vietnam is still weak in many aspects.

Road Transport

First we focus on road transport communications. There are fifty-one national highways throughout the country, with a total length of 11 535 km; 2777 bridges; and thirty-six ferries. The roads in the provinces' inland areas have a total length of 14 014 km, with 2793 bridges and eigthy-five ferries. In addition, there are 25 004 km of district roads; 2825 km of urban roads; 49 910 km of inter-community, inter-village roads; and 5451 km of special purpose roads. In general, with such a road network, and measured against quantity and a road–km index per unit of territorial area, then Vietnam is equivalent to other countries in the region. But from the quality point of view, Vietnam's road are generally in poor condition. Of the above total length of Vietnam's roads, only 12.7 per cent are asphalted. The remainder are broken stone or earth roads.

Based upon road design standards for road grades, at the time of writing, Vietnam has not yet built any Grade I roads; Grade II roads make up 0.63 per cent; Grade III roads, 31.6 per cent; and Grade IV roads, 34.9 per cent.

Regarding bridges, only 30 per cent of all the bridges can take a permitted tonnage of over ten tonnes.

Looking at transport by road, there are at the time of writing 41 500 trucks in the whole country (this number was 23 900 in 1985), with a circulated goods quantity of 2667 million tonnes per km. This number shows an annual average increase of 20 per cent.

As for passenger transport, there are in the whole country about 25 900 buses in the country, with 621 900 seats and a passenger circulation number of 10 601.3 million persons per km.

Railways

Regarding railways, there are 2600 km of main railway lines in the whole country, 840 km of spur railways and station roads, of which there are 2205 km of railways with a width of 1 m; 173 km with a width of 1.435 m; and 229 km with a width of 1 m + 1.435 m. In general, the Vietnamese railway system is still backward, with over 40 per cent of it not reaching technical standards; 40 per cent being narrow; and 20 per cent where rails should be replaced and sleepers superseded. The system of bridges, canals, tunnels, stations and communications is still inadequate, for many reasons, and does not reach required standards.

At the time of writing, Vietnam has over 485 locomotives with a total capacity of over 364 000 hp. The number of carriages is 5064, with a tonnage of 150 600 tonnes. As for passenger transport, there are 774 carriages, with 43 800 seats and an annual passenger circulation number of 1921 million persons per km.

Sea Transport

With a coastline of 3200 km and many favourable points at which build ports and quays, the state has not yet got a budget to invest in these. The sea signalling system is still inadequate and backward. On the whole coastline, there are thirty-five main lighthouse; seven seaports managed by central authorities; 7290 m quays; 2 207 000 m² of warehouses, and 476 000 m² of good yards.

As for the means of transport, there are 366 cargo ships, with a total of 617 900 tonnes, and the circulated goods quantity is 13 806 million tonnes per km. Passenger ships are primitive and in short supply. The annual circulated passenger number is estimated at 40 million persons per km.

River Transport

Because of its geographical position, Vietnam is a country with many rivers – to be more exact, about 2360 rivers and 41 900 km of canals. This is an encouraging factor for waterway communication development, but this potential has not yet been exploited. The waterway length in use at the time of writing is 11 400 km, 33 per cent of the total length of the river system nationwide. The numbers of means of transport on waterways is 915 tugboats of all kinds, with a capacity of 111 500 hp; 11 923 cargo ships and motor boats, with a tonnage of 188 600 tonnes; and 1663 barges, with a tonnage of 287 000 tonnes. The transported goods quantity of the whole waterway system is 2546 million tonnes per km, with 1310 million persons per km in passenger transport.

Air Transport

Vietnam's aviation system still has many limitations, and as a means of transport it is seriously lacking. There are some leased foreign aircraft and some others such as the TU-154 and TU-134 from the former USSR which are very old. The system of airports and airfields is very primitive. The circulated goods quantity is estimated at 19 000 tonnes per km, and the circulated passenger quantity at 1402 million persons per km.

In general, the transport and communications industry in Vietnam is still in a backward state, and is not yet meeting the socioeconomic development demands of the country.

OBJECTIVES AND SOLUTIONS FOR TRANSPORT-COMMUNICATION DEVELOPMENT IN VIETNAM TO 2010

Objectives

The objectives of transport-communication branch development in Vietnam are: overcoming dilapidation and gradually upgrading essential communication lines and works; investing in new construction work in a synchronized and modern way; modernizing communication works at border posts (international airports, seaports, important corridors connecting borderposts with inland areas, in main economic regions; and the north–south trunk-line).

Orientations and Basic Solutions

In the coming years, to reach the objectives of socioeconomic development to the year 2000, and the development strategy to the years 2010–2020, the transport and communication industry of Vietnam needs to concentrate on creating synchronization and co-ordination between main economic regions, communication links, and big cities.

During the process of strengthening and developing this material-technical basis, special attention should be paid to the study and application of scientific-technical advances, advancing gradually towards to the modernization and application of international technical indices where the necessary conditions have been met.

Up to the year 2000, intensive investment should be made in order to strengthen and upgrade the communication network and make full use of the existing material-technical base. In the development strategy of this industry, the road transport system remains the first priority as it has many strong points. So the strategy should concentrate on restoring and upgrading essential roads, building some big bridges such as the My Thuan bridge, the Quan Hanh bridge, and so on. Broadening and upgrading trunk roads, main streets and by-pass roads in Hanoi and Ho Chi Minh City. Upgrading roads in the border provinces and mountainous provincial roads leading to the centres of districts in remote regions. In general, the road network in Vietnam has been distributed evenly around the national territory. To ensure socioeconomic efficiency, there should be rational programmes for investing in strengthening and upgrading this system.

According to forecasts, by the early twenty-first century, road transport will be responsible for the transportation of 54 per cent of goods, and 80 per cent of transported passengers. Therefore, other means of transport in these areas should be investigated. Attention must be paid to joint ventures, which will help to establish and develop motorcycle and automobile assembly plants.

Maritime transportation development is another priority in the development strategy of the industry. Therefore, the strategic orientation for maritime transportation development of Vietnam is: to strengthen and increase the capacity of existing seaports; upgrade and enlarge the port of Haiphong; prepare and construct ports at Cai Lan, Chau May, Lien Chien, Dung Quat, Ben Dinh and Sao Mai; upgrade the port of Can Tho to become the central port of the Cuu Long delta; as well as to dredge rivers, improve river current flow and upgrade principal riverports to help the waterway system in the northern delta to handle barges of up to 1000 tonnes, and in the southern delta to receive ships with a tonnage of up to 2000 tonnes.

According to statistics, the national fleet can handle only about 20 per cent of the volume of imported and exported goods. Therefore, what should be done is to strengthen the physical infrastructure and renovate the industry's equipment. And other capital sources, together with investment capital from the state budget, should be mobilized and made full use of to build some large commercial ports.

To meet the increasing demand for transport, and to make it suitable for the receiving capacity of seaports and domestic goods sources in the future, special attention should be paid to investment in ships with a tonnage of 2000–5000 tonnes for coastal transportation, and sea vessels and river–sea ships in the south. Great importance should also be attached to the development of special-purpose ships for container transportation, oil tankers, and so on. Sea transport services and business activities should be organized to make full use of the existing resources, and negotiations should be carried out to sign maritime agreements with main partner countries.

Attention should be paid to the development of the road and bridge system in the deltas of the Hong river and the Cuu Long river and in the lake areas. Waterway transportation has an important position after road communications in Vietnam because of geographic and climatic characteristics.

In practice, river transport in Vietnam has great potential that has not yet been exploited because of a shortage of required investment capital and low transport charges. In the coming years, more attention should be paid to the development of waterway transport, especially to problems concerning river dredging, canal systems, river ports, quays, yards, warehouse systems, and so on.

The development objectives for waterway transportation aim to reach a capacity of one million tonnes; handle 33 per cent of the total transported goods in the whole country; and transport 172 million passengers.

The railway system plays a strategic role in Vietnam. However, its infrastructure and facilities are insufficient and very backward, and have not yet been replaced and upgraded as required.

The development direction for the rail transport in the coming years is to upgrade and reorganize the existing railway network, assuring safety and convenience in transportation; supply a system of semi-automatic signal information and mobile phones at larger stations to assure the safety for train management; prepare to build Hanoi–

HaLong–Ho Chi Minh City–Vung Tau railway network; and upgrade the north–south railway line through the Hai Van pass. The development of the railways must start from the strengthening and upgrading the existing infrastructure.

The railways aim to handle five million tonnes of goods and 36 million passengers by the year 2000. To realize these targets, the following have been estimated as necessary: there should be 6000 goods carriages, 2000 passenger carriages, and 2000 diesel locomotives, as well as strengthening and developing the Gia Lam train factory; the Saigon carriage-locomotive enterprise; the Da Nang locomotive depot; and the Di An carriage factory. There are studies on joint-venture co-operation to build a Trans-South East Asian railway line aimed at broadening the network as well as the transport capacity of the branch in the 'open-door' policy, and the development and integration of the national economy into the global economy.

Vietnam is in the process of establishing and developing a market economy with a socialist orientation. To realize this objective, co-operation and co-odination should be strengthened and enlarged. Demand for goods and passenger transportation by air has increased continuously. The aviation branch must satisfy all the demands set by the internationalization and modernization process, and stand firm before the sharp challenges of the market.

Aimed at meeting these future demands, the socioeconomic development task of the aviation branch was stated clearly at the 8th Party Congress as follows: 'enlarging and upgrading three international airports to help them reach modern standards with a capacity of receiving 12–13 million passengers per year. Upgrading airports of Cat Bi, Phu Bai, Nha Trang, Cam Ly, Ca Mau, and Can Tho. Opening new airlines, increasing the number of aircraft to meet the domestic and international demand for travelling by air'. To meet this development task, the aviation branch must rely on many sources and many different forms of ownership to reorganize and develop a suitable system of aircraft and special purpose facilities.

There should be a master plan for big provinces, cities and urban centres, to improve the infrastructure, establish a good public transport system, eliminate all points where traffic jams take place, and reorganize the signalling and traffic light system, and traffic control facilities. In the coming years, the transport-communication industry, with its many branches, will carry out the Instruction Nos 36, 39 and 40 issued by the prime minister and re-establish order on the roads, railways and waterways system.

The communication system in rural areas should be maintained, preserved, and upgraded with a view to construct and develop a 'new countryside'.

Developing the infrastructure for the transport and communication industry in Vietnam is now an urgent problem. A good and convenient transport system will create favourable conditions for implementing economic development objectives, shortening the gap between the different regions and areas in the national territory, and meeting increasing demand for goods transport and socio-cultural exchanges, as well as strengthening relationships with other nations in the region and in the world.

17 Vietnam Radio-Television: Investment and Business Prospects

Nguyen Anh Dung

LF2
B35 P 31

INTRODUCTION

Vietnam Radio-Television is a communication organ of the government of Vietnam. The Voice of Vietnam radio station came into being in August 1945, and the Vietnam Television station was officially operational after the country's reunification in 1975.

Currently, the Voice of Vietnam radio was transmitted to all fifty-three provinces, from nine broadcasting stations, reaching over 21 per cent of the area and 49 per cent of the population in 1994, and up to 40 per cent of the area by 1995. Total broadcasting time increased from 71 341 hours in 1991 to 175 000 hours in 1995, the yearly growth rate being 59 per cent. Total transmission hours increased from 21 000 hours in 1991 to 33 358 hours in 1995, the yearly growth rate being 32.5 per cent. In the period 1991–5, the state invested in the reconstruction of broadcasting installations but transmitting power was not improved because of insufficient capital (nationwide transmitting power was, in fact, decreased, from 2790 kW to 2560 kW).

There are now television stations in all fifty-three provinces in the country. Vietnam Television (VTV) broadcasts continuously from 6.00 am to midnight. Television transmitting power has increased considerably, from 45 kW in 1991 to 120 kW in 1995, with broadcasting time increasing from 5400 hours in 1991 to 8707 hours in 1995, a rise of 61 per cent. With nearly 300 transitional television stations, each day, 70 per cent of the population

in 60 per cent of the area can watch television programmes. There are four television channels: VTV1,
VTV2, VTV3 and VTV4.

RADIO-TELEVISION DEVELOPMENT
OBJECTIVES FOR 1996–2000

The Radio-Television objective to the year 2000 is to reach
95 per cent of the population with to the Voice of
Vietnam, and 80–85 per cent of the population with
national television programmes. The main development
directions are technological renovation, training and
retraining the workforce, and new investment in building.

Vietnam Radio-Television needs about US$115 million
for the five years 1996–2000 to invest in the construction of
broadcasting stations all over the country to enable it to
increase transmission time from 158 275.25 hours in 1995
to 386 647 hours in 2000.

The government of Vietnam has approved a project for
upgrading VTV stations, with a total capital of US$150
million. A project to build a new television centre in Hanoi
is being developed; a 350-metre television tower in the
West Lake area of Hanoi will be erected; and a transitional network with a capacity of 10 kW, 5 kW and lesser
capacity will be completed, to transmit programmes from
the central station to the localities. The modernization of
television installations throughout the country is being
carried out gradually by equipping them with Beta-Secam
system recorders and transmitters, and moving on to digitalization and the use of informatics in programme production procedures.

In recent years, the country's high economic growth has
improved people's living standards considerably, their
income has also increased rapidly. Together with the
increase in radio and television coverage area, the accelerating rate in the number of families having television and
radio receivers has greatly increased. Research data from
1993 shows that at that time 21.83 per cent of households

had TV sets, and 25.54 per cent had radio-cassette recorders. The market for electronic goods such as TV sets and radio-cassette recorders in Vietnam at the time of writing is extremely active. Besides traditional firms such as Sony, Sanyo and Panasonic (Japan), and Philips (Netherlands), newer companies such as Samsung and Goldstar (Korea) have also appeared. The market for audiovisual equipment is vigorous and will increase in the coming years.

VIETNAM'S RADIO-TELEVISION IN THE NEW INTERNATIONAL ENVIRONMENT

Prospects for Foreign Investment

So that by the year 2000, 95 per cent of Vietnamese households can listen to the Voice of Vietnam radio and 80–85 per cent can watch national television, it is necessary to accept that Vietnam must upgrade its television broadcasting quality to equal that of other countries in the region. All of these countries, including Thailand, Singapore, Malaysia, Indonesia, the Philippines, Hong Kong, Japan and China are applying new techniques to radio–television broadcasting. The technical solution of combining the Basys Automation System (part of a well-known US computing firm) with the D-crat Digital Audio-System of the ABC (Australia) is currently highly favoured.

The Voice of Vietnam radio has equipped its news centre with such a system, in common with nearly 500 radio stations in the world. In 1989, the governments of Vietnam and India signed a co-operation agreement on radio broadcasting. This was the first co-operation instrument signed officially by the Voice of Vietnam radio station. In July 1990, the Voice of Vietnam station signed a co-operation instrument with Radio Australia. This was the first agreement Vietnam signed with a Western country.

Vietnam Radio-Television runs professional training courses and seminars every year with assistance from such international organizations as UNESCO, UNICEF, and countries such as France, Australia and Canada. Hundreds of correspondents and editors trained in these courses have contributed their considerable talents to the renovation of Vietnam's radio and television broadcasting.

From 1991, Vietnam Radio began to develop an intensive co-operative relationship with Australia following the operation agreement to produce the programmes to teaching English: 'English Australia'. The general director of ABC radio has made several working visits to the Voice of Vietnam radio and the leaders of this station have been to Australia for exploratory visits. A large co-operative project costing about $A1.5 million has been operating from 1993 in which special equipment for three receiving–transmitting studios, each costing $A12 000 has been supplied, and ABC radio has helped in training correspondents and technical managers for Vietnam Radio–Television, with fifteen short-term training courses taking place in Vietnam.

Further, the station has also continued a SIDA project (Sweden) to assist some of the local radio stations such as Hanoi, Hue, Can Tho and so on, with a separate cultural co-operation agreement for the period 1996–8 worth 30 million Swedish Kroner (corresponding to US$5 million). This is aid for Phase II, to continue assistance to the Vietnam Cultural and Information branch, including the fields of radio, the press, and museum conservation.

There have also been regular radio-television exchanges and co-operation with correspondents, from Thailand, Indonesia, Malaysia, Singapore, Taiwan, Hong Kong, for example. The Voice of Vietnam radio station is an official member of the ABU organization (the Asian-Pacific association for radio and television, CIRTEFE). Since 1993, its representatives have regularly taken part the activities of this organization in New Zealand, Japan, Malaysia and other countries, with regional seminars and discussions about radio and television activities.

Vietnam's radio and television work has received assistance from several countries. Co-operation between Vietnam and Australia in this field has not so far been very great, but, in the future, Vietnam will need Australian's co-operation in the training of specialists and technicians, and in the upgrading of radio and television systems. During 1994–5, the co-ordinating committees of the two countries organized meetings and pushed for co-operation on technical training and the transference of radio technology at the central station as well as the upgrading of some local stations, and improving the teaching of English via the medium of radio. Some forecasts of planned radio and television transmission, state budget and required investment capital are given below in Tables 17.1–17.5.

Table 17.1   Radio and television transmissions 1996–2000, hours per year

	1990	1994	1995	1996	1997	1998
1 Broadcasting						
Total time of broadcasts	17 589	29 385	33 358	36 500	36 500	36 500
Total time of broadcasting frequency		179 108	175 019	192 600	192 600	192 600
2 Transmission						
Total time of transmitting TV programmes	2 300	3 900	4 901	6 205	7 665	7 665
The total time of transmitting TV frequency		6 000	8 707	10 324	15 300	15 300

Table 17.2   State budget on Transmissions, VN$ billions

A	Expenditure	29.1	337	445	575	617	811
1	Broadcasting				300	300	400
2	Transmission				275	317	411
B	Expenditure on general construction	20	80	250	873	777	1 403
1	Broadcasting				493	365	191
2	Transmission				380	412	1 212

Table 17.3   Investment capital demand for planned construction programmes by the Voice of Vietnam, VN$ million

Projects	1995 Plan	Demand				
		1996	1997	1998	1999	2000
Construction works of Groups A and B (Table 17.2)						
Editing and broadcasting technique	500	20 000	20 000	15 000	15 000	15 000
Northern broadcasting station	60 000	20 000				
Southern broadcasting station	60 000	20 000				
External broadcasting station		300 000	20 000			
Building FM broacasting station (local)		11 000	7 000	2 800	65 000	62 000
Building AM broadcasting station (local)			10 000	13 000	13 000	14 000
Aims of the programme						
To Provide information by radio transmission for listeners in the highlands, islands and rural areas	19 500	30 000	30 000	30 000	30 000	30 000
Total	140 000	401 000	107 000	60 800	123 000	121 000

Table 17.4 Planned television transmission in Vietnam, 1996–2000, VN$ millions

Projects	Source	Plan 1995	Budget 1996	1997
Construction works of Group A and B (Table 17.2)				
Projects for expansion of transmitting station network	Domestic capital	12 300	43 000	30 000
	Foreign capital	FF 20 mil.	FF 30 mil.	FF 25 mil.
Technical centre for Da Nang transmitting station	Domestic	2 000	8 000	2 000
Projects for improvement of transmission equipment		22 000	20 000	20 000
Planning, renovating and upgrading programme production, Centre I			7 000	6 000
Programme production, Centre II		500	40 000	57 000
Transmitting antenna tower		30 000	30 000	30 000
Local transmitting station		18 575	50 000	35 000
The aims of the programme				
Transmitting the image to highlands, border area and islands				
Total		125 375	258 000	230 000

Table 17.5   Total investment demand transmissions for in Vietnam, 1996–2000

Year	Expenditure (VN$ million)
1995	315 564
1996	380 928
1997	412 622
1998	1 212 196
1999	763 399
2000	800 000
Total	Investment demand 1996–2000: VN$3 567 billion

18 Vietnam and ASEAN: Relationships and Implications for Commerce and Investment

Nguyen Khac Thanh

375
P33
F14

F21

GENERAL INFORMATION

Economic relationships between Vietnam and the ASEAN countries before the year 1986 were not strongly developed. Vietnam's total export–import turnover in 1986 reached only US$120.1 million, of which as much as 70 per cent was obtained through bilateral trade with Singapore. In this period, relationships with COMECON countries in terms of commerce and investment played a dominant role in Vietnam.

Since the implementation of an overall open-door policy, Vietnam has changed its emphasis, concentrating on foreign economic ties with countries in the Asia-Pacific region. From this time, the ASEAN countries have played an increasingly important part in Vietnam's economy.

With Vietnam's membership of the ASEAN (from 28 July 1995) and its participation in the ASEAN Free Trade Agreement (AFTA) from January 1990, Vietnam's relationships with the ASEAN countries in the fields of commerce and investment have made a considerable steps forward, which are worth studying.

VIETNAM–ASEAN TRADE RELATIONS

Statistics show that the ASEAN countries account for 27 per cent and 32 per cent of Vietnam exports and imports respectively. In the period 1991–5, Vietnam's total export–import turnover with the ASEAN countries showed an average annual increase of 18–20 per cent, higher than that with other countries in the region. However, the expansion of trade relations with ASEAN has resulted in a great import surplus being suffered by Vietnam (which has seen the highest increase of all the import surpluses Vietnam has had with other economic regions) but brought about only a few changes to Vietnam's exports.

Excluding Singapore, the four remaining countries (Indonesia, Thailand, Malaysia and the Philippines) share only 10 per cent of Vietnam's total exports and imports, equal to the trade turnover that Vietnam has with Taiwan alone. This results from the fact that, economically, the complementarity between Vietnam and these four countries is at a very low level. The difference in terms of natural resources and technological development is smaller than that with Japan and the newly industrialized countries (NICs). The competitiveness of Vietnamese goods in the ASEAN market is not high. Vietnam's export–import turnover with ASEAN countries is shown in Table 18.1. Vietnam's main exports are raw materials and some farm products, while its imports include, for example, materials, semi-finished products, machinery and equipment. This has led inevitably to a fast-increasing import surplus.

Vietnam's participation in the AFTA will not help to boost its total trade turnover with ASEAN immediately, but will bring about a lot of benefits resulting from more balanced foreign trade exchanges – that is, the total trade with the ASEAN countries thanks to low tariff rates (under 5 per cent). Gradually, Vietnam will enjoy a growth in its exports to ASEAN member nations as a result of the fact that great exporters such as Japan, the European

Table 18.1   Vietnam's export–import turnover with ASEAN countries, per cent

Year	Exports	Imports
1990	13	19
1991	24.6	34
1992	21.5	37
1993	13	43

Union (EU), the USA, and NICs will take advantage of the trademark 'Made in Vietnam' to penetrate AFTA's large market of 420 million people. Vietnam's large labour force and low tariff rates will be the two main advantages, attracting multinational corporations to invest in the production of exportable goods in Vietnam.

Commercially, ASEAN countries will make full use of Vietnam's favourable geographical position to export goods to the potentially huge market of South China, with its population of 200–250 million people. As a result, Vietnam will have a larger import surplus with ASEAN but this does not mean that it cannot gain any profit from it. On the contrary, many benefits can be generated thanks to higher tariff rates imposed on ASEAN member nations' goods that are sold to the countries outside the block.

It is inevitable that the Vietnamese market will be flooded with goods made in other ASEAN countries. This may cause difficulties to domestic production at the beginning but will bring more benefits to Vietnam in the long term. This is the case because it will force Vietnamese enterprises, which have to face harsh competition, to improve production through advanced technology imported from countries outside the ASEAN in combination with lower labour costs. Thus it is possible that the competitiveness of Vietnamese goods will be increased thanks to the advantages offered by its AFTA membership.

ASEAN'S INVESTMENT IN VIETNAM

From 1988, when Vietnam promulgated a law on foreign investment until the end of June 1995, ASEAN's total investment in Vietnam reached US$2469.5 million, of which Singapore accounted for 50 per cent with US$1302 million; Malaysia with US$630 million; Thailand, US$305 million; Indonesia, US$163 million; the Philippines, US$67 million; and Brunei with US$2.5 million. ASEAN's investment made up 10 per cent of the total foreign direct investment (FDI) in Vietnam, which was not a small amount from the perspective of these ASEAN countries, who were also badly in need of FDI. Would FDI in Vietnam from those countries increase or decrease once Vietnam joined this association? The evidence so far is it has, up to the end of 1997.

Almost all of ASEAN's FDI in Vietnam during the years that the USA still maintained a trade embargo against the country was essentially made by US and Western European-originating firms. Therefore, it can be said that US and Western European enterprises have long established their foothold in the Vietnamese market. Since the normalization of relationships between Vietnam and the USA, some corporations from the USA, Western Europe and Japan have made big investments in Vietnam which exceed the FDI from ASEAN nations. Though there has not been a sharp growth in terms of quantity, FDI projects realized by ASEAN nations in Vietnam have developed at a fast pace, with some projects already operational, turning out products for local consumption as well as for export to a third country.

If Vietnam is granted most favoured nation (MFN) status by the United States it is likely that a considerable flow of FDI will move from ASEAN countries to Vietnam to take advantage of the possibility of penetrating the US market, which is considered to be a lucrative one. Moreover, some high-income countries such as Singapore and Malaysia, which may be deprived of their trade preferentials by the G7 nations in the year 2000, will also pour much of their FDI into Vietnam.

In relation to AFTA, the division among the ASEAN countries in the manufacture of some products will also lead to the movement of FDI into Vietnam to establish an optimum production structure. Besides, the fact that the intermediary Singapore port is overloaded may result in the possibility of investment in the upgrading of deep seaport services in Vietnam.

It is still too early to think of Vietnam's FDI in ASEAN countries. However, in the future (after the year 2010), when Vietnam has reached a certain development level and accumulated a certain amount of capital, this may generate investment possibilities in foreign countries to make use of their comparative advantages. At some point, Vietnam's FDI may appear in some ASEAN nations with a view to infiltrating markets that Vietnamese goods cannot penetrate directly.

CONCLUSIONS

It is likely that the relationship between Vietnam and the ASEAN in the fields of commerce and investment will see a lot of big steps forward in the future. Present statistics have not yet clearly shown these prospects, but it would be unwise to think that they are not worth researching. Therefore, it is thought that countries outside the ASEAN, especially Australia which has long-lasting ties with the ASEAN countries and is in the same region, should attach great importance to this research so as to gain the best outcome once they start to invest in Vietnam.

19 Vietnam's Manpower: NA Sources and Issues

ICTC staff

INTRODUCTION

Vietnam's sources of manpower come from the following areas.

Population and Source of the Labour Force

According to the 1989 Census, Vietnam then had a population of 64.4 million. The population has risen by some 12 million since then, as shown by Table 19.1. In terms of its population, Vietnam ranks twelfth in the world, with a natural growth rate each year of about 2.2 per cent. Attempts by the government to reduce this to around 1.7 per cent with a policy of 'one wife, one child' have met with some success to date.

Among the 76-odd million people, about 45 per cent are under 15 years of age. Thus Vietnam belongs in the category of 'young population' countries. Being a populous

Table 19.1   Population figures, Vietnam, 1990–6

Year	Population
1990	66 233 300
1991	67 774 000
1992	69 306 170
1993	70 800 000
1994	73 000 000
1995	74 400 000
1996	76 400 000

country, the labour force in Vietnam is an abundant one. Nearly 45 per cent of the total population are working people in different branches of the national economy; among them, 24 million (or 33 per cent of the population) are in the agricultural labour force, and some 5 per cent are in the industrial labour force. The state sector covers 4 per cent, with some 3 million people while the private economic sector covers 40.5 per cent, about 30 million people.

It was estimated that, up to the end of 1995, there were among the above working people, 4 million basic technical labourers; over 12 million, with a secondary education; over 700 000 a high school level education; and nearly 10 000 a master or doctoral level of education.

In addition, Vietnam has a powerful contingent of overseas Vietnamese-born citizens amounting to some 2 million people throughout the world, a large proportion of whom have qualifications in scientific and technical fields. In recent years, overseas Vietnamese have contributed an active part to the building and economic development of the nation.

At present, Vietnam also has more than 200 000 of its nationals living and working abroad, mainly in Russia, in former East European countries and in some Asian countries like Korea, Japan, and so on.

From an assessment by foreign experts, Vietnam's source of manpower is not only plentiful but the workers are also industrious, skilful, well educated and quick to acquire advanced science and technology.

JOB PROVISION IN RECENT YEARS

With the pressure of a fast-rising population, the number of working people has increased continuously every year. In the 1975–80 period, the increase was 3.37 per cent a year; in the period 1980–5; 3.38 per cent; and in 1985–90; 3.55 per cent. It is expected that the 1990–2000 period will see an annual increase of 2.58 per cent, and after the year

2000, 2.05 per cent. Up to the year 2000, the number of people seeking jobs will increase by some 6 million, so some 1.2 million new jobs will have to be created each year. The abundant source of manpower has been a precious asset to the country, especially in times of war. But now, the job problem is a burden that demands an early solution.

According to a survey carried out in 1996, the unemployment rate in Vietnam's urban areas was on average over 6 per cent, which means that there were 2.5–2.6 million unemployed people; among them, young people account for nearly 70 per cent. This is a high rate; an alarming level that surpasses the limits of social security insurance. Meanwhile, joblessness in rural areas is also at a serious level. The regional localities that use 50–70 per cent of available labour time in arable areas are also gradually shrinking because of the urbanization process. From calculations by economists, people without a job now amounted to some 6 million people. The countryside's working people who are now flowing into the cities to seek jobs have created 'labour markets' in the big cities such as Saigon and Hanoi, and this rural labour force is worsening existing unemployment in the cities.

A noticeable aspect of the labour market in Vietnam in recent years is the shortage of highly skilled cadres. The open-door policy of the national economy has encouraged direct investment by foreign countries in Vietnam in recent years. This has created jobs mainly for the highly skilled and professionals. A large part of the highly skilled labour force is being switched from state-owned and collective enterprises to foreign and private companies. Because of the gradual loss of professionally experienced cadres, domestic companies are facing deficits and are on the brink of bankruptcy. Workers of a low professional level either have to leave their jobs temporarily or move to other fields of activities. This further aggravates the number of people unemployed.

Faced with this situation, Vietnam has in recent years applied a number of measures, and has to some extent eased the tension over joblessness. One of the measures has been that regarding population and family planning, the most important national programme. Thanks to this measure, the rate of natural population growth reduced from 3 per cent in 1993 to 2.2 per cent in 1995. The programme of population movement (in inner and outer regions) has brought about a rational population and labour apportionment, while the exploitation of natural resources has created more new jobs. (Programme No. 327 alone moved more than 230 thousand households and over 1 million inhabitants, and created jobs for nearly half a million of workers.)

On 11 April 1992, the national fund for job provision was set up. This fund has loaned the people nearly VN$1 billion, with preferential conditions, assisted nearly 20 000 people with small-scale projects, and created jobs for a million people. Different humanitarian aid programmes (from the former Czechoslovakia, Germany, the European Community and the High Commission for Refugees) have created conditions for reintegration and provided jobs for more than 200 000 of those repatriated. However, the provision of jobs for workers still needs appropriate measures, in both the immediate future and in the long run.

ORIENTATION AND NECESSARY MEASURES IN LABOUR AND JOBS

To eradicate the old concepts about jobs, to make every citizen understand that in whatever economic component or branch and wherever they are working, they should feel comfortable with it, provided the job is useful to the society and to themselves. As well as this, the state must solve problems of a macroscopic and strategic kind.

1. Jobs and the use of multi-manpower technology. There should be an appropriate policy to attract foreign investment. There should be a clear distinction of key branches and skills that need to have invest-

ments in high technology. There should also be an emphasis on various branches and skills that are poorly technically equipped but that use more manpower and serve the needs of domestic consumption, together with making products that could compete on the world market. Together with modern equipment, the policy should use more human resources to build infrastructure (roads, bridges, for example, and branches that attract more labour force in Vietnam at present, such as the fields of agriculture, forestry, clothing manufacture, and so on.).

2. Temporary jobs. To provisionally accept those jobs that have low productivity, or below-average productivity in society, but which would contibute to an increase in GNP. Seen from the aspect of the individual and their families, such a solution helps in the immediate resolution of the job problem, as well as psychological and social/ethical problems.

3. Social policy regarding finance and the law should encourage an appropriate environment for creating jobs; create conditions for free mobility of labour; attract capital among the population, and support family planning programmes, for example.

4. There should be a policy of linking the problems of labour and jobs to the strategies of socioeconomic development, and to specialized and targeted programmes; to organize training and retraining; to popularize branches and skills for working people to have job opportunities or create jobs for themselves; to build a national job programme, considering it to be an important means for developing source of human resources; in the immediate future, to aim at the exploitation of underdeveloped and job-producing regions such as the Mekong river delta, the northern midlands, the Tay Nguyen highlands, and the southeastern zone; and to develop urban and concentrated industrial areas, thus striving to reduce, by the year 2000, the rate of unemployment to 4 per cent, and by 2005 to 3 per cent.

There should be a flexible policy to attract foreign investment with a view to developing the national economy, and providing more jobs at home while exporting some of the labour force abroad.

The population–labour–jobs problem will still be a burning social problem of the first priority into the early years of the twenty-first century, a factor that has a great influence on the process of socioeconomic development in Vietnam. Nevertheless, the state of Vietnam has been able to draw on a lot of useful experience to find a solution to this problem. With a huge potential in terms of natural resources, and with an abundant source of labour, the state has created, and continues to create, appropriate policies to encourage the development of production, to stimulate all citizens to enhance their existing capabilities; to broaden new branches, skills and fields; to campaign for birth control to reduce the rate of natural population growth, closely linked to other policies in foreign affairs; and to take care of qualitative labour force development in both its physical and spiritual aspects to meet the requirements of national industrialization and modernization.

HUMAN RESOURCE DEVELOPMENT PROSPECTS IN VIETNAM

In 1995, Vietnam and Australia signed an agreement to initiate human resource development in Vietnam, with both countries exchanging ideas about the matter. The Vietnamese have suggested sending cadres to Australia to research industry, forestry management, and the development of marine products.

Being a country with an abundant labour force, Vietnam very much wishes to have investment, both public and private, from Australia to help solve its labour problems. On the other hand, Australia is a country of large capital resources, of modern production technologies, and of rich natural resources, so it could import labour from Vietnam, especially to work in those fields that need more manual labour.

In order to raise the quality of human resources, Vietnam needs assistance from Australia regarding multi-skilled training. Australia can send lecturers to Vietnam to train Vietnamese cadres, or create conditions for Vietnamese people side to study in Australia.

Such co-operative relations between these two countries in the field of human resource development in Vietnam offer the potential of a great deal of mutual benefit for the future.

At the more general level of human research develop-ment (HRD) research and policy formulation, other inter-national organizations such as the UNDP and the ILO have recently been interested in these issues in Vietnam. This interest will surely continue to be an important aspect of future work on labour, job markets, and other HRD issues such as unemployment, training, retraining and reskilling in Vietnam, which is a major developing and transition country in the ASEAN and East Asia. Foreign expertise is greatly needed in this area especially in the context of economic integration and globalization.

20 Official Development Assistance (ODA) Programme

Nguyen Khac Thanh (Vietnam) 019 P33 F35

INTRODUCTION

Before 1991, Vietnam received official development assistance (ODA) from two main sources: countries under the COMECON (which essentially were the former USSR, and Eastern European countries), and capitalist countries such as Sweden, Finland, Denmark, Norway, India, Kuwait, for example. The total amount of ODA received up to 1991 was US$21.150 billion. Additionally there was US$1.6 billion from other multilateral finance sources (such as the IMF, ADB, WB, for example). A considerable part of ODA and multilateral finance funds was received by the South Vietnam administration and noted down in the debt accounts of the reunified Vietnam after 1975.

In general, during the pre-1975 period, the ODA capital funds for the regions of the North and South Vietnam were aimed essentially at military objectives. Only 20–22 per cent of total ODA financial assistance funds were estimated as being directed towards civil objectives. From 1975 to 1991, the ODA funds from the COMECON countries were directed to economic development objectives, especially to the fields of infrastructure construction and industrial works. A considerable part was spent on directly imported consumer goods such as food, fuel and so on.

The event of the collapse of the USSR and the Eastern European countries in 1991 ended the ODA sources of Vietnam from them. The US embargo continued until the end of 1993, and this prevented support from other ODA sources, although there were a few countries (principally the North European countries and Australia) which continued to maintain ODA financial assistance to Vietnam.

In 1993, Australia re-established its ODA programme to Vietnam (see Table 20.1). After the lifting of the US-imposed embargo, the USA did not prevent multilateral aid to Vietnam, and since then ODA and other multilaral financial assistance funds have been rapidly and continuously increased, surpassing the receiving capability of Vietnam (1994: US$1.86 billion, 1995: US$2.1 billion). Up to 1995, the most important matter was not the mobilization of the ODA funds, but the effective use of the financial assistance.

ODA CHARACTERISTICS TOWARDS VIETNAM

In general, towards Vietnam, ODA has the following characteristics:

On the Scale of ODA Funds

Between 1993 and 1995, Vietnam signed agreements with foreign sponsors valued at US$4.6 billion, of which Japan offered the most, with US$1275 million; the World Bank (WB), US$1118 million; the Asian Development Bank (ADB), US$634 million. (Through the Conference of Sponsors, the total undertaken ODA capital was US$1.86 billion and, within a year, with regularized documents, it had reached US$1.464 billion – equal to 78.7 per cent.) This was a big step forward in the attraction of ODA capital to Vietnam, but it is still on a small scale. For example, in the case of Israel, ODA from the USA alone was US$3billion, while with Egypt, it was US$2.4 billion.

Over the past few years, implemented ODA was estimated at about US$1.7 billion, out of which there have been a number of large projects and programmes funded, such as:

- Credit for correcting structures   USD 90 million
- Credit for restoring the countryside   USD 52 million

Table 20.1   Aid targets towards Vietnam at the Conference of
Sponsors, November 1993, US$ millions

Bilateral ODA source	Project	Programme	Foods	Assistance	Total
Australia	51.4			28.9	70.3
Belgium	5				5
Canada	10				10
Denmark	11.8	1.5		1.5	14.8
Finland	6.9				6.9
France	64.4			19.2	83.2
Germany	26.1			19.4	45.5
Italy	10.6				10.6
Japan	430.5	108.1		12.0	550.6
Korea	57.2			2	59.2
Malaysia				0.4	0.4
Singapore				7.5	7.5
Sweden	10.3			10.8	30.0
Switzerland				6.7	6.7
Thailand				2.0	2.0
United Kingdom	75.5			26.4	101.9
Subtotal:					1 004.6
Multilateral ODA source					
ADB	220.3	80.1		12.0	312.5
EU	45.2				45.2
IFAD	22.5				22.5
UNDP				25	25
UNFPA	8				8
UNICEF	25.0				25.0
WB	275.0	125.0			400.0
WFB			13.0		13.0
WHO				5.0	5.0
Subtotal:					859.0
TOTAL	1 361.3	314,7	13	171.3	1 860.0

Source: The World Bank, *World Debt Tables 1994–95*.
Notes: ADB = Asian Development Bank; EU = European
Union; IFAD = International Fund for Agricultural Development;
UNDP = United Nations Development Programme;
UNFPA = United Nations Population Fund;
UNICEF = United Nations Children Fund; WB = World Bank;
WFP = World Food Programme; WHO = World Health Organization.

- Countryside programmes   USD 40 million
- Goods supporting programme   USD 10 million.

ON THE STRUCTURE OF ODA CAPITAL FUNDS

Because of the difference in sponsors' objectives, the structure of ODA capital invested in different branches in Vietnam is also very different. When analysing ODA capital sources over the past few years, it is possible to make some preliminary observations, as follows:

- Bilateral supplying funds have a density higher than multilateral supplying funds. More specifically, of the total US$1860 million of ODA capital funds, bilateral funds are US$1004.6 (equal to 54 per cent), while multilateral funds are US$850 million (making up 46 per cent). The programmes and projects sponsored by non-governmental organizations make up US$170.8 million (equal to 9.87 per cent).
- In the form of bilateral ODA capital, Japan is the greatest aid source, representing 29.6 per cent, while, in the case of multilateral aid, the World Bank has the biggest share at 21.5 per cent.
- Aid capital according to projects has a highest density: US$1361.3 million (67.8 per cent), followed by aid according to the programmes: 16.9 per cent; and the remainder is essentially bilateral technical aid.
- Almost all ODA capital funds are connected to the projects and large-scale projects (involving over US$100 mollion). In our calculations, in 1995, the total executed ODA capital was about US$900 million, of which the capital for large-scale projects made up over 70 per cent, essentially concentrated on infrastructure and the four fields of: transport; communications; hydraulic energy; and water supply and drainage. Together with infrastructure were the programmes for 'Hunger Eradication–Poverty Reduction', and education.

- To every ODA sponsor, the structure of finance is also diversified. For example, the World Bank has signed three important credit agreements with Vietnam:

  (i)   Primary education project   US$70 million;
  (ii) Agricultural restoration   US$96 million; and
        project
  (iii) National highway 1A   US$158 million.
        restoration project

While with the UNDP, through four national programmes, the ODA also reflected a diversified structure, as follows:

(i)   National Programme No. 1 with a total capital of US$49.08 million (17 projects);
(ii) National Programme No. 2 with US$64.5 million (55 projects);
(iii) National Programme No. 3 with US$107.29 million (108 projects); and
(iv) National Programme No. 4 with US$104 million (93 projects).

These projects cover many fields. There are, for example, nineteen projects approved, costing US$19.5 million. Law projects comprise: a law on minerals (VIE 92/009), and a law on gas and oil (VIE 94/011). Strengthening the judicial capacity (VIE 94/003) received a total capital of about US$2 million.

Management projects comprised: land management (VIE 94/006); economic management training (VIE 93/004); and strengthening urban area management (VIE 94/006). Other projects are: rearing freshwater fish (VIE 93/001), a subterranean work map project; and a supporting project, for example.

It should be noted that no substantial project dealing with the social outcomes of Vietnam's economic reforms in a regional, national or international context has been supported by these organizations to date.

Through a number of agreements signed in recent years, it is possible to observe the diversified character of ODA projects and programmes, but when they are considered in a branch context, industry is always the branch with a greatest density: 25.39 per cent of the total ODA capital, while agriculture, forestry and irrigation have only 12.15 per cent, and transport and communication, 14.62 per cent. The other remaining branches share 47.84 per cent.

THE ROLE OF ODA TOWARDS VIETNAM IN THE PERIOD 1996–2000

While ODA has always played an important role in Vietnam, it now has ever more importance and significance. It is well known that to reach economic growth naturally investment capital is needed. The correlation between growth and investment capital is expressed in the form of the coefficient ICOR (that is the rate relating investment capital to added value arising from investment).

To increase average income per capita twofold by the year 2000 compared to that in 1990, we must, following the calculations, assume the coefficient ICOR to be: 3–3.5, and should then have an estimated sum of investment capital of over US$50 billion. Domestic capital funds can only provide about 50 per cent of this amount; the remainder must be sought in the form of foreign investment capital, a part of which is ODA capital (while a relationship can be estblished between ODA capital and FDI capital, it should be carefully calculated in the usage).

In recent years, Vietnam's international relations broadened, and as a result, the attracted ODA funds have increased and played an active role in many socioeconomic fields.

In the field of macroeconomic management, there are many projects and programmes of international organizations, specially of the UNDP and the World Bank helping Vietnam to implement structural reforms and to speed up the process of changing to a market mechanism.

In the economic branches, ODA capital has contributed to the acceleration of development.

In the field of energy, ODA capital funds have been invested in the construction of many large-scale power plants. Some of these are, for example, the thermo power plants of Phu My 1, Phu My 2, Pha Lai 2, the Ham Thuan–Da My hydro power plant and Song Hinh and some other plants which are pressing for the completion of plans for construction. Together with the construction of hydro power and thermo power plants, ODA support has transformed the electricity network system in some cities such as Hanoi, Hai Phong, Nam Dinh, Hue and Ho Chi Minh City, together with some countryside areas.

In the communications field, ODA capital funds have been used to support countryside telecommunications and telephone switchboard projects, enlarging the mobile communications system of Hanoi–Hai Phong–Quang Ninh, Hanoi, the Ho Chi Minh City switchboard project and the Tay Ninh province switchboard project. A number of projects, have been completed and brought into operation, thus improving the telecommunications service of Vietnam.

In the fields of agriculture and irrigation, many projects have been planned and developed, including some important projects such as the project to restore of the Bac Thong–Do Luong system; the Hanoi dikes; irrigation development projects for the central provinces (such as Thanh Hoa, Nghe An, Ha Tinh, Quang Nam–Da Nang, Quang Ngai and Phu Yen) and Ho Chi Minh City; the An Giang irrigation project; and irrigation projects for five northern provinces (Ninh Binh, Nam Ha, Thai Binh, Hai Phong and Quang Ninh).

In addition, there are a number of programmes related to the countryside or rural development to restore some basic crops such as rubber, sugar cane, and, particular, tens of thousands of hectares have been reforested by using ODA capital funds.

In the sociomedical and cultural fields, ODA capital funds have also helped to transform and upgrade the water supply–drainage system in some major cities such as Hanoi, and Ho Chi Minh City, and some other urban area, plus small towns in the provinces. In the years 1993–5, ten thousands of funds were set up in the countryside areas to support a clean water supply.

In the medical field, many big hospitals such as Cho Ray Hospital (Ho Chi Minh City) and nine other hospitals in Hanoi have been transformed and supplied with modern equipment using ODA capital. A major project for strengthening primary healthcare has been agread, and other programmes on population and family planning; preventive measures against goitre, malaria, and AIDS; inoculations, and so on have been developed.

In the training and educational field, ODA capital funds have also supported postgraduate training in some overseas countries, short-term training in foreign languages, and professional techniques for a number of officers, as well as a primary education reform programme, the provision of school equipment, and so on.

Technical support projects have also been developed as these projects have a strong influence on many other projects in the socioeconomic field.

Some preferential fields attracting ODA capital the indicated below. From Government Decree No. 20/CP dated 15 March 1994 promulgating the ODA using management statute and Circular No. 7 UB/KTDN dated 18 July 1994 of the State Planning Committee (now the Ministry of Planning and Investment), we note the following preferential directions.

With non-refunding ODA, priority should be given to the following fields:

- Medical and sociocultural problems. Priority areas are the supply of medical equipment; upgrading constructing medical bases of all kinds; supplying further medicines; implement population and family planning programmes; and health care and epidemic disease prevention programmes.
- Strengthening the capability of education and by training bases, transforming, upgrading or providing further machinery equipment to serve all training needs; providing regular in-service, long-term and short-term training.

- Giving priority to programmes of hunger eradication and poverty reduction, implementing humane programmes, creating jobs, overcoming some social diseases, and social evils, improving material and spiritual conditions of accommodation, restoring cultural works, and developing sport and gymnastic activities.
- Dealing with environmental protection problems: priority should be given to programmes related to environmental protection, and the management of urban areas.
- Science-technology. Priority should be given to programmes aimed at strengthening the ability to study and apply in some important science-technological fields, to problems of technology transfer, and to co-operation.
- With budget supporting problems: Reserving preferential conditions to programmes of importing consumer goods for domestic use or importing foreign currency to help the account balance of the state budget.

With re-funding ODA, Priority should be reserved for the following:

- Programmes relating to energy: the construction or transformation of power plants; and transforming the system of electricity transmission and distribution.
- Upgrading and constructing new roads, railways, waterways, bridges, ports, airports, and particularly urban traffic.
- Supporting the development of credit in the countryside, the agricultural product processing industry, and agricultural encouragement. Supporting the creation of disease-Resistant plants and animal breeds; and developing, transforming and upgrading irrigation systems.
- On socio-economic infrastructure: it depends essentially on non-refunding ODA. It must pay attention at the same time to some other problems such as primary healthcare, university centre construction, education reforms, and so on.

ODA AND AUSTRALIAN AID

Australia has agreed two undertakings to supply ODA capital to Vietnam with an amount of $A62 million for the period 1991–4, and $A200 million for 1995. The structure of the aid was as follows.

Training

Providing training for officers of the Ministry of Education and Training, the Ministry of Planning and Investment, the General Department of Aviation, and the Ministry of Justice.

Infrastructure

Project relating to the 500 V power transmission line (Ministry of Energy); the law on construction (Ministry of Construction), North My Thuan Bridge (Ministry of Transport and Communication), sugar cane supply to the provinces of Ha Tinh, Bac Giang and Tra Vinh (Ministry of Construction), transforming the Chief Architect's Office into the Planning Department (People's Committee of Hanoi City); a studying on water at An Giang; and urban planning at Da Nang and in the south.

About Medical Problems

Projects on malaria prevention, healthcare, and upgrading a number of hospitals in Nghe An, and Nam Ha. Programmes of community health, eye inspection, and so on.

All programmes sponsored by Australian ODA have been operating well. However, while the investment rate for consultiation, training and the provision of expert help is good, the capital available for other items in the projects is small. The following appraisal of some Vietnamese experts has been advanced: Australian ODA programmes in Vietnam have not been directed as yet to all objectives in Vietnam that need them. In fact, some irrational distributions of ODA funds from Australia have taken place. In the future, ODA funds coming to Vietnam from Australia are expected to increase. So, to use this kind of capital effectively, the governments of the two countries must assign the priority to vital areas, and complete the consultation period well before any investment is made.

CONCLUSIONS

ODA capital (together with FDI) is the foreign capital having great importance in the country's development. In Vietnam in its period of renovation, has experienced difficulties in the attraction of such capital, because it is not a limitless source. Vietnam is in a crisis situation and is facing strong competition in the international capital market.

With the renovation policy and achievements in both domestic and foreign economic fields, however, Vietnam has opened up new opportunities and expectations towards the attraction of foreign capital, of which ODA capital is a part.

To attract and use this capital effectively Vietnam should continue its renovation work, implement the planning direction of management renewal correctly, avoid waste and corruption. At the same time, it should be aware of the problem of external debts that can put great pressure on the country policy and direction of development.

Bibliography

Communist Magazine, April 1994.
Decree No. 20/CP on 15 March 1994 and Statute of Management and Use of ODA, Office of the Government of Vietnam.
International Monetary Fund (1995) *World Economic Outlook*, October.
World Bank, *World Development Report: 1992, 1993, 1994*.
World Bank, *World Debt Tables 1994–1995*.

21 Trade, Investment and Business in Vietnam: Issues in Development and Operation

Tran Van Hoa

In the preceding chapters, detailed information and a sound analysis of the conditions of the local demand for and the local supply of trade, investment and business (TIB), and other co-operation in Vietnam have been provided by noted writers in their relevant areas of expertise. The conclusions we can derive from this information and analysis indicate that there is a huge surplus of demand over supply, and Vietnam, at this stage of its economic development, cannot meet it alone. Ample opportunities exist for trade, investment and business for foreign corporations and individual investors.

Even when opportunities exist, how to develop the areas of TIB, how to promote them, and how to operate and manage them involve more effort than would be expected; this is true, of course, of all businesses, be they local or international.

In the case of international TIB, things are necessarily more complicated even for countries with a similar history, cultural make-up or language. For international TIB in foreign, developing and transitional countries such as Vietnam, things are necessarily more complicated. This does not mean that doing business in Vietnam is a no-win situation. The proof is simple: while some international investors and corporations have lost their money and their (ill-founded or too hastily formed, perhaps) faith in doing business in Vietnam, others have made their fortunes there, both in the short and in the medium term (Vietnam's reforms, as we are aware, started only around 1988).

While it is feasible to do an analysis detailing the reasons why Vietnam has been known as a graveyard for many businesses (as stated by HE Susan Boyd, Australian Ambassador to Vietnam at the Darebin City Networking Meeting, Melbourne, February 1996), it is also feasible to do an analysis detailing the reasons behind the financial success of such corporations as the ANZ, Telstra, Gateway, Vabis, and numerous other Australian and international companies doing business in Vietnam. This work is, however, beyond the scope of the present book.

From a robust and analytical standpoint, however, the success of a business, or for that matter of any other human endeavour, depends on the accuracy and timeliness of the information about that business being available and properly used. To be able to use this information judiciously and to predict future trends or movements of the business reliably is sometimes a gift of a good business acumen, a result of advantageous inside or extraneous information, sometimes sheer luck, or simply a result of hard work, thorough investigation and sound deduction. The last is fundamental in the top-down or bottom-up approach to foreasting the movement of share prices in stock market studies. It is also the basis for predicting the effect of monetary policy on the economy as used by the Reserve Bank of Australia, or predicting the effect of fiscal policy on the economy as used by the Treasury (or the government).

In this context, the preceding chapters are an invaluable source of information on trade, investment and business in Vietnam, and with it, the subsequent opportunites for Australian and other foreign corporations and individuals to develop trade, investment and business there. It is also more than that. The chapters, as part of their presentation structure, provide in many cases official or semi-official forecasts on the sectors they are dealing with to up to the year 2010 or even 2020. These forecasts have been made by experts in the various government ministries and departments where the contributors to the book have official appointments. They are in this sense forecasts of future trends and directions in the sectors, and they are as reliable as one can get.

Developments of trade, investment, and business in Vietnam based on this kind of information and its expert analysis would invariably produce fairly accurate opportunities for good corporate planning and policy formulation. This is an important objective of the present book.

Index